gardening with Old Roses

JOHN SCARMAN

gardening with Old Roses

JOHN SCARMAN

HarperCollins*Publishers*

For Teresa
without whose support and wonderful photographs this
book would not have been possible

First published in hardback in 1996 by HarperCollins*Publishers*
This paperback edition published in 1999

99 01 03 02 00
2 4 6 8 9 7 5 3 1

All photography by Teresa Scarman
Garden illustrations by Simon Buckingham
Pest and disease illustrations by Brian Hargreaves (except red spider mite,
page 139, and leaf-rolling rose sawfly larva, page 139, © Amzie Viladot;
leaf cutter bee, page 140, by Denys Ovenden)

A CIP catalogue record for this book is available from the British Library

ISBN 0 00 414085-0

Text set in Perpetua and Gill Sans
Colour reproduction in Singapore by Colourscan
Printed and bound in Italy

The HarperCollins website address is:
www.**fire**and**water**.com

Contents

AUTHOR'S INTRODUCTION

Canon Hole, in his delightful *Book about Roses* written in 1874, sums up the whole subject thus: "He who would have beautiful roses in his garden must have beautiful roses in his heart. He must love them well and always. He must have not only the glowing admiration, the enthusiasm and the passion but the tenderness, the thoughtfulness, the reverence, the watchfulness of love." It is because I share such feelings about Old roses that I have chosen to work with them and I have written this book in order to share my enthusiasm and fascination with other people.

Scents can evoke memories for many people and one of my strongest childhood memories is of my grandmother's garden, which smelled of rosemary, juniper and roses. I am sure that my fascination and love of roses stems in part from these early memories. Working with roses, I developed a fondness for the old varieties in particular and had a strong desire to conserve these lovely plants. This led, in 1983, to settting up our nursery, Cottage Garden Roses, which would concentrate on 140 of the best Old roses, and by limiting the number available to the most highly recommended varieties, make old-fashioned roses more accessible to people.

In 1986 we decided to make a formal rose garden in our nursery at Woodlands House, which is also where we live. We were at a slight loss as to how to approach the design for what had to be both a show garden and a family garden combined. We enlisted the help of garden designer Jane Fearnley-Whittingstall with whom we had had several happy collaborations in connection with the Chelsea Flower Show. She came up with the design for the beds and together we decided to underplant the roses with herbs and fragrant perennials. The reasons for this were twofold: firstly artistic, with the

companion plants complementing and enhancing the colour and texture of the roses. Secondly, planting roses in association with other subjects avoids many of the pests and diseases associated with growing only one type of plant. We have become fascinated by plant associations and show some of our successful ideas in the chapter on Planting with Old Roses.

In a formal rose garden, where consideration must be given to the proportions of the beds, it would be inappropriate to allow untidy growth and presentation, however artistic, to destroy the balance, so regular pruning of the roses is vital. Many people have admired our garden in winter, after it has been pruned, for its neatness, symmetry and architecture. In late spring, before the roses come into flower, the borders and arches are a rich tapestry of different shades of green. And largely as a result of the success of our

(left) The formal rose garden at Woodlands House is planned to show the public as many different rose varieties as possible. Designed by Jane Fearnley-Whittingstall, it has a formal, symmetrical layout, the rose beds edged with clipped santolinas.

(right) Old roses are excellent subjects for cutting and arranging. If the flowers are picked at different stages, from tight bud to half-open blooms, this gives the appearance of the roses as they are seen in nature and also prolongs their vase life.

own garden, I have become involved in designing rose gardens for other people and advising on the reconstruction of existing ones. The chapter, Designing with Old Roses, and the pruning and practical sections of the book, covered in Caring for Old Roses, have been written entirely from experience.

One of the keys to planting and designing with roses is the correct choice of variety. But with over a thousand roses to choose from, this might appear to be a daunting task. In this book I have deliberately limited the choice of roses to 150 varieties in order to make the selection process easier. This is very much a personal selection and, like any exercise of this nature, will of course invite criticism of both inclusions and omissions. But this book has been written with the gardener firmly in mind and seeks to answer all the questions, both practical as well as about the choice of variety, that we have so often been asked.

The question I always dread being asked is "What is your favourite rose?" The answer I have to give is that they are all individuals, with their own distinct personalities and, like our four children, I would not choose between them.

John Scarman

designing
with Old
Roses

DESIGNING WITH OLD ROSES

The great Renaissance gardens of Italy and France were designed to show man's dominance over nature, and flowers were used as single jewels to adorn the built design. In the eighteenth century the symmetry and formality of these gardens were swept aside by the more naturalistic style of the English landscape movement, in which flowering plants had little part to play. By the latter part of the nineteenth century, however, plants were once again in fashion, thanks both to the foreign introductions of plant finders, and to the strides that were being made in hybridization and propagation – in North America and in other parts of the world, as well as throughout Europe.

Grander gardens, with their head gardeners and rows of underlings, were elaborate, productive, time-consuming affairs, and cottage gardens of course continued to exist. But a new breed of gardener was appearing: men, and especially women, who not only cared about gardening but were interested in the theory of it, in the use of colour and texture, in the way plants were displayed, and in the history of the plants themselves. Gardeners like Gertrude Jekyll and later Vita Sackville-West not only wrote about gardens but actually worked in them. Their aim was essentially to create informality of planting within a framework that would set off the plants to their best advantage. It was symmetry with a paradox.

The revival of interest in Old roses was largely due to Gertrude Jekyll, and we would do well to follow her precepts when gardening with these wonderful plants. Old roses, when properly pruned and presented, epitomize the voluptuous and the romantic in gardening. Such is their diversity of style and habit that you will find an Old rose for virtually every position in the garden, from 'Pompon de Bourgogne' as a formal, clipped edging, to the great billowing 'Complicata' free-standing in an orchard, and a choice of neat Climbers or tumbling Ramblers to provide height and interest on a garden structure.

CREATING THE FRAMEWORK

The ideal situation for growing roses (which few of us have) is an open aspect in the proximity of trees to offer shelter and coolness. But whatever the nature of your garden – and the overall pattern and shape of the garden is less critical than people think – it is important to work out a ground plan before you start to plant. You need to plan the size and shape of the beds, the position of paths

This garden, designed by Mrs Jane Stevens, is a fine example of a rose garden in keeping with the period and style of the house.

(be generous with both, or the outline will be rapidly lost as the planting matures), and the position and height of any garden structures. But keep the design simple: good planting is, with these roses, even more important than the plan. In the same way, one well-presented structure in the garden will be more effective than a fussy collection of smaller ones – and this will, of course, also make the pruning of your Climbers considerably easier.

Paths between beds of Old roses can be made of any natural, or high-quality imitation of a natural, surface: gravel (honey-coloured gravel looks good with roses), brick, stone (or reconstituted stone) slabs, setts, decking or even old railway sleepers; it is only the more glaring modern concrete slabs that look inappropriate.

A successful garden design depends on three things – good proportions, balanced and sympathetic planting and finally, but of equal importance, appropriate pruning of the plants in it. Many a great garden does Old roses a disservice because of the widely held and erroneous belief that these roses need not be pruned. Rather, they need to be pruned according to their needs, and different groups need different pruning to give of their best. I describe the pruning methods I recommend in the section on pruning in Caring for Old Roses (see page 106).

It is far easier to work out a new planting scheme than to change an existing one, and it pays to be ruthless with existing planting. It requires courage to pass the death sentence on old plants, but remember that even large plants can be moved in the autumn, provided they are pruned to balance the root loss. If you move Old roses, mark the spot with a cane and do not replant with a rose in the same place.

(above) The screen of rose arches acts as a garden divider, allowing glimpses of the planting beyond.

On the arches are 'Gloire de Dijon', 'Sombreuil', 'Céline Forestier' and 'Madame Isaac Pereire'.

(left) This arch is planted with pink-hued roses. 'Madame Grégoire Staechelin' is the first to come into flower, followed by 'May Queen' on the left. The companion is the blue-flowered solanum, kept tightly pruned.

(above) This delightful mixed border, edged with the rose 'De Meaux', is planted with roses and other plants including delphiniums, white foxgloves and lychnis, which soften the solidity of the stonework. If the planting was too dense, it would obscure the attractive old stone wall completely.

Planting heights are graduated from ground level (R. × richardii) up to 7ft (12.5m) ('Alba Maxima').

Standards of 'Hermosa' give height. to this small border, planted to suit a cottage garden.

CHOOSING THE ROSES

Once you have drawn up your ground plan, you will be able to choose roses from the Directory to match the position. And this is the secret of successful planting: to choose the rose to suit the site. You should look at the roses' height and width, their flowering time, their preference for sun or tolerance of shade, their tolerance of exposed positions or need for shelter – and, of course, at their colour. In the garden there will be some key planting areas: those that are the first to be seen from the house; those that lead the eye to a feature; those that surround a bench or adorn a structure; those on the corner of a bed. These will demand repeat-flowering roses.

Colour, of course, is very important. Remember that white and the lighter colours show up best at a distance, so use the darker ones nearer the house. Use Old roses in colour drifts, avoiding fruit salad effects, and change subtly from one colour to another, using structural plants to link them together. In beds of mixed planting do not let one colour predominate – beware, especially, of blues and yellows. On large structures like pergolas or tunnels, opinions are divided on whether a single colour of rose should be used, or several. If you decide on the latter course, change the colours slowly along the length.

When grouping roses in beds, you should consider not only the colour of the flowers, but also the size and shape of the blooms, whether they are double or single, once-flowering or repeat-flowering. Some of the larger-flowered roses can overwhelm the delicate beauty of their smaller relations if planted in too close proximity.

Old roses can be used in many ways – in beds, as hedges, as great flowering mounds, to cascade down a bank and to cover a wide range of structures and boundaries. Ramblers like 'Paul's Himalayan Musk'can be used to soften the outline of buildings or garages, and to cover old trees.

Blaikie, a slightly cantankerous Scots gardener, living in Paris in the 1770s, noted in his diary that the French 'look upon a house and a garden as two objects that do not correspond with the other'. Today's thinking is that the garden should complement the house both in period and in atmosphere. The partnership between Gertrude Jekyll the gardener and Sir Edwin Lutyens the architect reflected this harmony. However, a light touch in the planting is often sufficient to bring things together. For example, a yellow room could have yellow Climbing roses around the window, and some yellow roses in the planting viewed from the windows; anything more would tend to upset the colour balance in the garden as a whole.

Some garden designers insist on using plants dating from before that of the house. This seems to me less important than designing in a way that is sympathetic to the house and its surroundings. Old roses will enhance any garden, and it would be a pity to exclude the many wonderful herbaceous plants that are available today.

OLD ROSES IN BEDS

Old roses do not lend themselves to the regimented, formal plantings of the Edwardian rose garden; they are essentially informal, romantic plants and the way they are used should reflect this. Far fewer plants will be required than would be the case if you were using Hybrid Teas, and it is important that the grouping of the roses is carefully considered. Plants of one variety in a group or drift should be planted so that when mature

(above) Stone slabs on the edge of the lawn facilitate mowing and allow the planting more space. 'Albertine' on the wall is enhanced by the airy Crambe cordifolia.

(left) Beds which do not have a retaining edge have a more informal, natural effect.

(left) Edging the formal rose beds with dwarf box hedges increases the crisp formality of the design. 'Madame Hardy' is planted in the beds.

(left) *The billowing and romantic planting makes full use of the wall to bring height and impact. Drifts of R. mutabilis are offset by the lower-growing sage, rue and lavender.*

(right) *'Madame Alfred Carrière is used to camouflage the modern brick wall. Noisette roses do this particularly well, provided they are regularly pruned.*

they grow into each other, giving the appearance of a single specimen of very generous proportions; those of the next variety should nearly touch the first, but allow for companion planting between (see Planting with Old Roses, page 35). Old Shrub roses that grow to a height of up to 3ft 6in (1m) should be planted in a group or drift of four plants; those that grow up to 4ft (1.2m) in a group of three; the larger shrubs in twos. It will take about three years for the plants to reach maturity, and annuals such as clary (*Salvia viridis*) and the annual gypsophila can be used in the first year, provided they are not allowed to arrest the growth of the roses.

There is also the question of underplanting. Beds all of one colour are not usually underplanted, while mixed beds generally are.

You need to decide whether you will edge your beds and, if so, whether with low box hedging, a hedging of roses or an alternative (see rose hedges, page 123) or with brick, tiles, slate, stone or tanalized wood. If you are using hedging, you will not be able to plant right up to the edge, and the effect will be far more formal.

ROSES ON WALLS

The choice of a Climber is dictated by the colour and height of the wall, as well as by the overall scheme of the garden. As a general guide, the Teas, Hybrids Teas and Bourbons are quite sparse in growth, with fewer flowers, so it is important to decide whether you want to complement or match the colour of the flower to that of the wall. For example, the dark red of 'Guinée' could be used to splendid effect against a grey stone wall, while a pale yellow brick would be enhanced by the yellow and pink shading in 'Gloire de Dijon'. The foliage of the Noisettes and Ramblers, on the other hand, is far more dense, and since the flowers are held against the foliage the colour of the wall behind is less critical. However, a white-flowered Rambler like 'Félicité et Perpétue', with its small flowers and thick foliage, will always look dramatic and pretty against a white wall. Small-flowered Ramblers, and Climbers like 'Noisette Carnée' ('Blush Noisette'), can be grown against almost any background, and all are hardy enough for shady walls. Just avoid too strong a contrast: a dark red rose against

a white wall, for example. In general, the brighter colours and stronger contrasts of large-flowered Climbers are best used furthest from the house.

The next consideration is the height of the wall. A wall under 8ft (2.5m) in height is best planted with a Rambler like 'Albéric Barbier' which grows horizontally, or, if space is limited, with a Shrub rose, for example one of the Hybrid Musks; *R. × alba* 'Alba Maxima', 'Celestial' or 'Tuscany Superb' would also be good choices. It does not matter if a wall at this height does not catch the sun; you need not choose a particularly shade-tolerant plant unless there is overhead shading from trees as well.

On walls over 10ft (3m) in height, whether the aspect is sunny or shady can be important, though this is perhaps over-stressed. The more tender varieties may suffer if they are grown against a cold, sunless wall, but most Rosarians tend to recommend roses for shady walls on the strength of their ability to flower well in low light conditions rather than for their hardiness.

A difficult planting position is one between two ground-floor windows, and here a tightly clipped planting of

'Lord Penzance' or of *R. primula* can introduce a delightful perfume throughout the house. If a taller rose is needed, the early pale yellow *R. banksiae* 'Lutea' is a great favourite, and can be trimmed during the summer, after flowering, for a neat appearance.

You may wish to plant your wall with climbing companions for the roses (see the chapter on Planting with Old Roses, page 43, for ideas).

OLD ROSES ON FENCES

Here the habit of the rose is important. Hybrid Teas like 'Madame Caroline Testout' and Ramblers like 'Bobbie James' send out strong vertical shoots which would soon become unsightly. A good choice for covering a wide area, at least 15–20ft (4.5–6m), would be a Rambler like 'Léontine Gervais' which has a pendulous and horizontal habit. For a shorter length, 8ft (2.5m) or so, the Hybrid Musks would give a delicate cottagey feel, and will flower in trusses all summer long.

(*right*) *The trellis arch is planted with 'Zéphirine Drouhin' (on the left) and 'Blairii Number Two' (on the right), with purple plants such as alliums, sages and lavenders at its feet. The gate allows an expansive view of the countryside beyond.*

Larch lap fencing can be broken up by trellis panels in a dark colour (green is particularly good), placed alternately against the fence panels along its length, to give more depth and interest. Plant the roses on the blank fence panels between the trellis-covered ones.

OLD ROSES FOR GARDEN STRUCTURES

Tall structures such as tunnels, arches, pergolas and gazebos give height and interest in the garden and are an excellent way to display roses. Care needs to be exercised in how they are placed: they should be an integral part of the garden and link together elements of the design. Standing on their own, without any relationship to other features, they can appear quite incongruous.

The proportions of any structure are important. They should not be too mean, but nor should they be so large that they dominate the garden. It is a good idea to make a mock-up using tall bamboos to see what impact the structure will have and at this stage any adjustments can easily be made. If the structure is too low, it may cut through the view of the garden. Its height and width should be balanced and, in a pergola at least, they should be the same. Consider the structure from all sides to make sure that it is in keeping with the house and the rest of the garden. The path under a structure should always lead somewhere, to a bench or a statue, for example, or simply to a large container or other feature acting as a focal point.

'Sombreuil' grown with claret vine on trellis.

'New Dawn' covering a stone architectural feature.

(right) The steel arches are joined together with swags to form a light and airy tunnel. Planted with 'New Dawn', the tunnel is equally attractive viewed from the side. The sundial positioned at the end of the tunnel forms an attractive focal point.

(above) This series of metal arches is planted with 'Madame Isaac Pereire' and a claret vine (Vitis vinifera 'Purpurea'). Pruning for a neat and precise effect is essential on metal structures such as this.

(below) Just enough of this enchanting stone arch, planted with the vigorous 'Wedding Day', has been left to capture the imagination. It allows a tempting glimpse of the water beyond.

Tunnels, Arches and Pergolas

A pergola or tunnel is designed to lead somewhere, and should have the area around it planted up so that it does not appear too isolated. It should always be solid and well built, made either of wood or steel; there is little point in training roses carefully over a structure that will quickly disintegrate. A tunnel is usually made of steel and a pergola of wood. With steel there is no need for fancy scroll work, since the growth of the roses will rapidly hide it. The simplest classical look is sufficient. Wherever possible, avoid any tubular steelwork as this usually corrodes internally. Wood can be almost as expensive a material as steel, in relation to its durability. Tannalized, pre-treated timber is the best option and the upright posts should be a minimum of 3in × 3in (7.5cm × 7.5cm), with the top rails 3in × 2in (7.5cm × 5cm), set on edge.

The proportions of a tunnel or pergola are important, and if you are having a structure made by a blacksmith it is worth having a good sketch drawn up to work to, which will show the distances between the bars and hoops and the height from the ground at which the curves start. The structure should be at least 6ft (1.8m) wide, to allow two people to walk side by side, and at least 7ft (2.3m) high in the centre. The posts should be set to form a series of box sections, equidistant apart in all directions, and it is useful to have galvanized wire stretched at 18in (45cm) intervals across the top to help train in young growth.

The tradition with tunnels and pergolas is to plant the roses equal and opposite (see Planting and Establishing Roses, page 134), but this convention can be challenged by having roses of a similar colour, for example 'Gloire de Dijon' and 'Céline Forestier'. A tunnel requires formal planting and detailed pruning, which means using Climbers or the neater Ramblers like 'Noisette Carnée' ('Blush Noisette') or the Barbiers 'Albéric Barbier' or 'Léontine Gervais'. A pergola, on the other hand, asks for a less tidy, more romantic effect, and Climbers and Ramblers can be mixed. Here, the larger Noisettes like 'Madame Alfred Carrière' and 'Desprez à Fleurs Jaunes', or the Hybrid Tea 'Madame Grégoire Staechelin' could be grown with the Barbiers or with 'New Dawn'. For these structures, flowers of a pendulous habit are obviously an advantage.

Rose arbours and gazebos are private, even secretive places to sit, and the planting should be both romantic and scented. On smaller structures such as these, roses such as 'Blush Noisette' or 'Phyllis Bide' could be used.

Large, free-standing structures are far colder than walls, and to clothe them properly you should ensure that a vigorous variety is chosen, or it may not fulfil its promise. For example, for a pink effect, 'Madame Caroline Testout' or 'Blairii Number Two' would be a better choice than 'Zéphirine Drouhin'. Nor is it reasonable to expect Bourbons or Teas to cover a structure more than 8ft (2.5m) high by 8ft (2.5m) wide. To be on the safe side, for a 6ft (1.8m) structure choose a variety that will grow to over 10ft (3m) on a wall, and follow the guidelines on pruning (see page 106).

(above) This oak pergola, curved to follow the line of the wall, is a magnificent piece of joinery. It is planted with 'Adelaïde d'Orléans'.

(left) Swags are most useful as garden dividers since they do not reduce the feeling of depth nor do they cut off the view. Here, Multiflora roses are seen embellishing a dark background.

SWAGS, PILLARS AND OBELISKS

Swags of roses are created by chains or ropes suspended from poles. There are two ways of doing this: with the roses suspended above the ground or leading from the pole to the ground and then up to the next pole. Swags, popular in France in the nineteenth century, can be used to frame entrances, emphasize walks, or accentuate different levels in the garden. Being quite delicate, they do not impede the view beyond. Use Ramblers with a pendulous habit, like Barbier Ramblers and Sempervirens.

Pillars are best planted with one rose on either side, whereas obelisks usually require only one rose to be planted in the centre. Both require neat and detailed pruning, and this limits the choice of variety to Gallicas, Bourbons, Hybrid Musks and the small repeat-flowering Ramblers like 'Mrs Billy Crick'. Historically, Ramblers were used for pillars, and their pliable stems

In informal planting, it is important to select the roses for their ability to be left unpruned. Choose varieties such as 'Paul's Himalayan Musk', seen here growing up a fruit tree in the orchard.

corkscrewed around them. Shrub roses cannot sustain the contorted growth and should be tied in vertically. Where pillars and swags are used together, a delightful combination is to grow Ramblers like 'Léontine Gervais' on the swags, and Hybrid Musks like 'Cornelia' on the pillars.

You can also grow roses on low ropes to enclose a seat or a grass area. Ramblers like 'Albéric Barbier' or 'New Dawn' work well for this, and could be underplanted with a low herbaceous plant like the blue catmint (*Nepeta*).

ROSE HEDGES

Roses make an excellent subject for hedging, and they are surprisingly versatile in their uses. For low edging, roses with small leaves and flowers, like 'Pompon de Bourgogne' and 'De Meaux', can be used; for a 6ft (1.8m) garden divider, 'Complicata' would be excellent, with its large madder single flowers followed by autumn hips. As with most hedges, the density of foliage and neatness of habit are vital in a formal situation, and since this will depend to a great extent on the pruning, the summer pruning of repeat-flowering varieties, as well as the winter pruning of both, must bear this in mind. It is important to prune rose hedges to a batter, with the top of the hedge narrower than the bottom (see the section on pruning hedges, page 123).

Mixing varieties in a hedge does not usually work unless the roses are identical in habit: for example, you could use several varieties of *R. rugosa*. Even then, such a hedge is better on a boundary. Rugosas are ideal for a roadside as they can resist the pollution from vehicle emissions, and from de-icing salt.

A hedge can be a useful device in making a transition from one style to another: either between one part of the garden and another, or, in the country, between the garden and a field, where a hedge of dog roses (*R. canina*) could be planted. It is also worth remembering that Rambling roses can be planted on low ropes to give a hedging effect.

WILD GARDENS

Rambling roses and fruit trees consort well together in orchards , provided very vigorous varieties like 'Bobbie James' or 'Kiftsgate' are not grown over too small a tree. As a guide, use Noisettes like 'Madame Alfred Carrière' and medium-sized Ramblers on trees under 20ft (6m) high; Musk Ramblers like 'Rambling Rector' on trees 20ft–30ft (6m–9m); and 'Kiftsgate' on those over 30ft (9m).

Mown paths meandering through long grass studded with wild flowers will provide a delightful, low-maintenance effect, and in the clearings tall, free-standing Shrub roses, which need no support or pruning, can be planted. Favourites for this are 'Complicata', 'Fritz Nobis', 'Wolley-Dod' (*R. villosa* 'Duplex'), 'Agnes' and dog roses (*R. canina*). For really large and spectacular effects you could plant Ramblers like 'Paul's Himalayan Musk' to create huge mounds up to 15ft (4.5m) high and 25ft (7.5m) across. Simply start the Rambler inside a split fencing support 4ft (1.2m) high by 6ft (1.8m) across; it will require no further attention and the long shoots will mound on top of themselves. If this is done down a bank it will achieve the effect of a cascade. I recently planted 'Adelaïde d'Orléans' at the top of a quarry to look like a white waterfall.

ROSES AND WATER

There is an enchantment about the association of roses and water. Even the smallest expanse will reflect the flowers, especially those of plants that are not too upright in habit. By choosing ones with

a laxer growth, you can achieve the effect of roses cascading into the water.

The use of water in gardens dates back far earlier than gardening in Europe. The Moguls used it extensively in early Persian gardens; it was also an important element in Islamic gardens. And in European gardens of the Renaissance, fountains, moving water and the sound of water were all much used.

Whether you have a long, formal, rectangular pool or a country pond, roses can always be planted in association with it. Your canal could be used to divide two long beds of roses and other border plants; a runnel or millstone water feature could have Old Shrub roses strategically placed beside it; and your country pond or stream could have larger, more voluptuous Shrubs planted alongside.

The best roses to use with water are those with a slightly untidy habit, which will need little pruning. Most of the Old once-flowering varieties, like *R. × richardii* or 'Stanwell Perpetual', will do well on the edge of a stream or pond, provided the roots are not waterlogged.

(top left) *'Complicata' surrounds the duck pond. The flowers always look enchanting seen against dark water, where reflections have been created.*

(top centre) *When 'Buff Beauty' needs to be tidied up, the only practicable solution is to prune it from a boat.*

(top right) *Ramblers in profusion tumble over a low wall and into the water.*

(above) *White-flowered Ramblers, including 'Bobbie James', are seen rambling through the existing trees and reflected in the water alongside the rustic bridge.*

THE MODERN VILLAGE GARDEN

The formality of the first half of the garden, with its symmetrically planted beds, gives an invitation to go through the arch to the more informal end. The view from the house through the arch and to the arbour beyond gives the garden a sense of depth and interest. The construction of the arch and trelliswork divider is not elaborate, nor does it make use of expensive materials since the foliage and habit of the Climbers clothing it will make a dense screen. The wood is stained to look like dark oak.

The paving beneath the arch, like that of the patio, is built from honey-coloured pavers with a natural stone finish. The edges of the beds are raised one brick high, the bricks matching the colour of the house. Brick is the ideal material to use in a curved design, its small scale enabling it to be laid in a curved line. Woven wooden boundary fences surround the garden; they have been stained to give texture and horizontal training wires are fixed to them every 18in (45cm). The choice of Ramblers is influenced by the need to give fast-growing, dense cover over the boundary fences.

Viewed from the house, the planting is bright and colourful, with the white of 'Sombreuil' and the solanum framing the pink-clad arbour at the end of the garden. Yellow Ramblers frame the sides of the garden against which the dark colours of 'De Rescht' and 'Madame Isaac Pereire' stand out dramatically.

THE MODERN VILLAGE GARDEN

This small garden, *20ft × 30ft (7m × 10m),* has an open aspect and receives sun from mid-morning until the evening. It is planted to give the appearance of width by the symmetrical use of the roses on opposite sides. The half of the garden nearest the house is like a 'room' and the gates set in the entrance arch can be closed to give a feeling of privacy, while still allowing a view of the garden beyond. The rose varieties in the beds in the second half of the garden are not matching although the colours chosen are similar and balance each other.

THE TOWN GARDEN

The lower part of the garden is planted with China and Polyantha roses to provide delicate-sized flowers, offset by an underplanting of herbs. An expanse of green lawn separates the similarly planted beds on either side. The roses in urns on the steps – 'Baby's Blush' and 'Little White Pet' – have been chosen for their repeat-flowering and their suitability for pot culture.

The grass banks are cut only infrequently to allow the texture of the longer grass to emphasize the change of level.

The informality is carried further by planting *R. × richardii* at the top of the bank to tumble downwards.

It would be wise to install a trickle irrigation system in this garden at the outset since town gardens tend to be more enclosed and therefore hotter than those surrounded by countryside. Town gardens will generally come into flower earlier, so care needs to be taken with feeding the roses, giving sufficient organic liquid fertilizer to cope with the extended flowering season.

Though the garden is generally maintenance-free, the pergola itself requires a lot of detailed work. Shoots need to be tied in or pruned as appropriate and regular deadheading is required to ensure a succession of flowers.

The planting on the pergola has been chosen to give as long a flowering period as possible: it is clothed in flowers from spring onwards, with the white-flowered wisterias, then the summer roses, followed by the late-flowering Ramblers.

THE TOWN GARDEN

This symmetrically designed town garden is 40ft (13m) long by 30ft (10m) wide. It is intentionally detailed and fussy to make the most of the small plot. The pergola is intended to give a cool and cloistered feel to this small urban garden and to add a sense of perspective. This is enhanced by the flagstone paving and the change of level, with shallow steps halfway along the garden. The cobblestones under the pergola itself create a different texture at ground level and make an interesting feature which can be seen from the house in winter.

just touch each other when in flower without being crammed in to such an extent that they are in competition for food and light.

The orchard has six fruit trees, including damsons, apples and plums, with rambling roses growing through them. The grass in the orchard is deliberately left long, appropriately for a wilder area of the garden. The lower hedge is made of dog roses, pruned twice during the course of the summer.

The path to the front door is one of the main features of the garden, enclosing a secluded arbour on one side and hiding the transition to the orchard on the other. Gravel, which is an appropriate and reasonably priced material, is now available in a wide range of colours. The pale honey-coloured shades look best with old-fashioned roses. If the budget allowed, blue engineering bricks laid in a herringbone pattern would make an attractive alternative.

The planting in the beds on either side of the curved path is full of roses and other old cottage-garden favourites, such as alchemilla, artemisia and foxgloves. The colours have been selected to form drifts in harmonious groups.

KEY TO VEGETABLE GARDEN

- (48) Tomatoes
- (49) Turnips, parsnips
- (50) Sweet peas on tripods
- (51) Herbs (chives, parsley, sage and thyme)
- (52) Salad (lettuce, radish, spring onions)
- (53) Strawberries, gooseberries, redcurrants
- (54) Line of 'Comte de Chambord' (cut flowers for house)
- (55) Runner beans
- (56) Compost heap
- (57) 'Rambling Rector' (over shed)
- (58) Potting shed
- (59) Greenhouse

THE COTTAGE GARDEN

One of the delights of cottage gardens is that there are no hard and fast rules. However, the planting in this garden mainly consists of harmonious drifts in the same colour, interspersed with more structural plants such as *Sidalcea* and *Campanula*. The texture of the foliage and the size of the flowers are important to the overall balance.

The planting in a cottage garden should be dense enough to prevent any patches of bare earth. Ideally the plants should

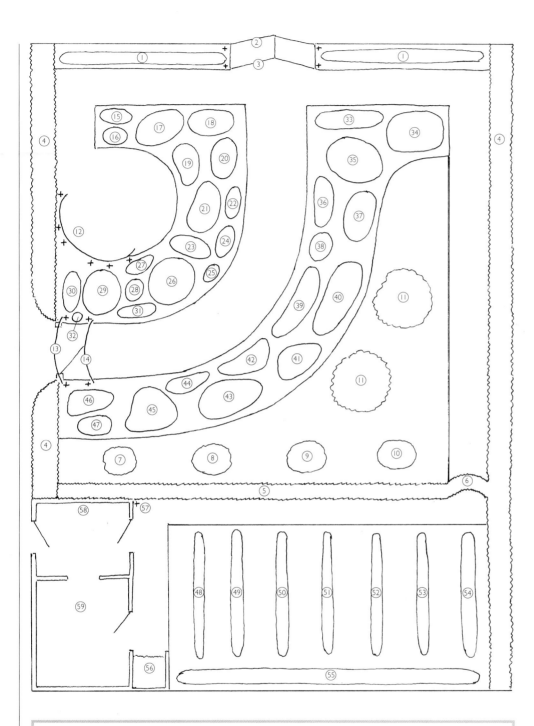

KEY TO PLANTS

1. 8 × Lavandula × intermedia *'Grappenhall'*
2. Clematis *'Ville de Lyon'* (on both sides of the porch)
3. *'Zéphirine Drouhin'* (on both sides of the porch)
4. Beech hedge
5. Hedge of Rosa canina
6. 2 × *'Bleu Magenta'* (either side of the arch)
7. Plum tree with *'Albéric Barbier'*
8. Damson tree with *'Madame Alfred Carrière'*
9. Apple tree with *'Léontine Gervais'*
10. Pear tree with *'Desprez à Fleurs Jaunes'*
11. Apple trees with Ramblers through them
12. Rose arbour (from top left: *'Variegata di Bologna'*, Clematis *'Perle d' Azur'*, *'Veilchenblau'*, *'Veilchenblau'*, Clematis *'Perle d' Azur'*, *'Variegata di Bologna'*)
13. 2 × *'Gloire de Dijon'* (on both sides of rose arch)
14. 2 × *'Céline Forestier'* (on both sides of rose arch)
15. 2 × Gypsophila paniculata *'Baby's Breath'*
16. 2 × Campanula persicifolia alba
17. 2 × *'Moonlight'*
18. 2 × Dianthus *'Mrs Sinkins'*
19. 2 × Lupinus *'The Governor'*
20. 2 × Artemisia *'Powis Castle'*
21. 2 × *'Jenny Duval'*
22. 2 × Verbascum creticum
23. 2 × Digitalis purpurea
24. 2 × Geranium *'Johnson's Blue'*
25. 1 × Salvia superba *'Blue Queen'*
26. 2 × *'Fantin Latour'*
27. 1 × Calamintha grandiflora
28. 1 × Lupinus *'Chandelier'*
29. 2 × *'Golden Wings'*
30. 2 × Brachyglottis *'Sunshine'*
31. 4 × Tanacetum parthenium aureum
32. 1 × Bupthalmum salicifolium
33. 3 × Dianthus *'Gran's Favourite'*
34. 4 × Sidalcea *'Sussex Beauty'*
35. 3 × *'Félicité Parmentier'*
36. 2 × Penstemon *'Alice Hindley'*
37. 2 × Campanula lactiflora *'Prichard's Variety'*
38. 2 × Catananche caerulea
39. 2 × Salvia purpurea
40. 2 × *'Ferdinand Pichard'*
41. 3 × Digitalis purpurea alba
42. 3 × Meconopsis cambrica
43. 2 × *'Buff Beauty'*
44. 4 × Origanum vulgare aureum
45. 3 × R. gallica *var.* officinalis
46. 2 × Nepeta *'Six Hills Giant'*
47. 1 × *'Complicata'*

THE COTTAGE GARDEN

The best cottage gardens are pretty and productive, with full, tumbling flowering plants offset by neat lines of vegetables. The overall shape of this design is characterized by generous beds and paths, since intricate and fussy details often become obscured when cottage-garden planting matures. The main garden lies in front of the house and the vegetable plot runs along the plot's front boundary.

THE ROSE GARDEN

The rose garden in this country plot is intended as a surprise, secluded yet at the same time offering glimpses through the 'windows' cut into the yew hedge. The colours of the roses stand out in sharp relief against the dark green of the yew. The hedge acts as an effective wind-break and at the same time traps the perfume of the roses. A narrow gravel path runs next to the yew hedge to act as a barrier, preventing the yew roots from invading the rose borders. An alternative would be to bury galvanized sheeting about 2ft (60cm) deep between the yew hedge and the rose garden. An area of gravel also runs underneath the entrance arches.

The colours of the roses planted on the arches and in the beds are equal and opposite, so that a degree of symmetry is achieved through the use of colour, from whatever angle the garden is viewed. The roses on the arches need to be regularly deadheaded (according to the variety) to retain a formal and symmetrical appearance.

The formal effect of the planting is heightened by an edging of clipped dwarf cotton lavender (Santolina chamaecyparissus 'Nana') which emphasizes the curve of the inner circle. The theme of a circle within a square was very popular in early designs. The height of the central sundial or fountain is carefully judged to emphasize the circular design.

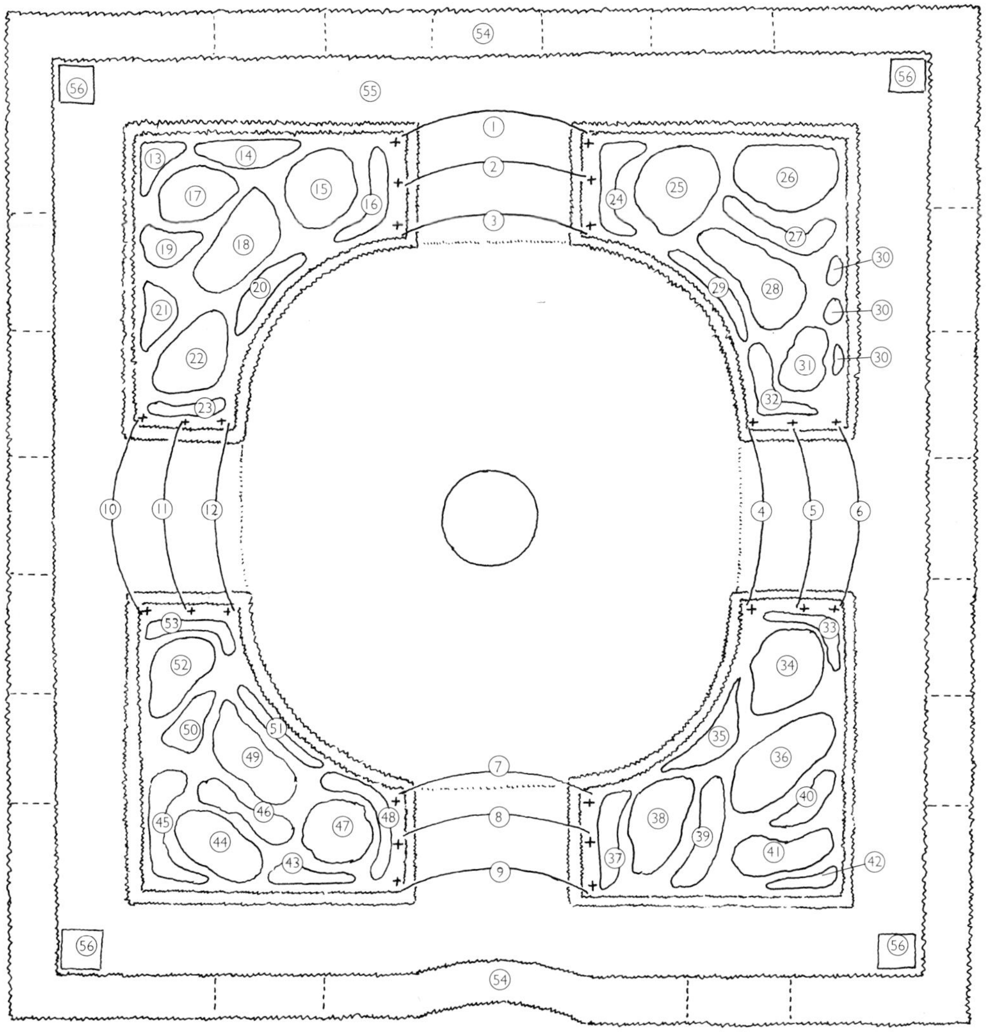

THE ROSE GARDEN

This formal rose garden is enclosed by yew hedging and approached through an arched entrance. 'Windows' have been cut into the hedge here although, depending on the location, more entrances could be added in place of some of the windows.

KEY TO PLANTS ON ARCHES

① 2 × *'Tuscany Superb'*
② 2 × Lonicera periclymenum *'Belgica'*
③ 2 × *'Reine des Violettes'*

④ 2 × *'Céline Forestier'*
⑤ 2 × Lonicera periclymenum
⑥ 2 × *'Phyllis Bide'*
(all of the above are planted on both sides of arch)

⑦ 2 × *'Veilchenblau'*
⑧ 2 × Vitis vinifera *'Purpurea'*
⑨ 2 × *'Madame Isaac Pereire'*

⑩ 2 × *'Sombreuil'*
⑪ 2 × Lathyrus latifolius albus
⑫ 2 × *'Gloire de Dijon'*
(all of the above are planted on both sides of arch)

KEY TO PLANTS

⑬ 2 × Alchemilla mollis
⑭ 2 × Geranium magnificum
⑮ 2 × *'Belle Amour'*
⑯ 3 × Sisyrinchium striatum
⑰ 2 × *'Rosa Mundi'*
⑱ 2 × *'De Rescht'*
⑲ 1 × Phlomis russelliana
⑳ 2 × Artemisia stelleriana
㉑ 2 × Aster amellus *'King George'*
㉒ 2 × *'William Lobb'*
㉓ 2 × Digitalis purpurea
㉔ 3 × Salvia sclarea *var.* turkestanica
㉕ 2 × *'Mevrouw Nathalie Nypels'*
㉖ 2 × *'White Pet'*
㉗ 2 × Digitalis terruginea
㉘ 2 × *'Souvenir de la Malmaison'*
㉙ 2 × Aquilegia vulgaris *'Nora Barlow'*
㉚ 3 × Inula hookeri
㉛ 1 × *'Daybreak'*
㉜ 2 × Ballota pseudodictamnus
㉝ 3 × Santolina pinnata *subsp.* neapolitana
㉞ 2 × *'Camaïeux'*
㉟ 3 × Salvia purpurea
㊱ 2 × *'Jenny Duval'*
㊲ 3 × Lavandula spica
㊳ 2 × *'Reine Victoria'*
㊴ 2 × Achillea millefolium *'Moonbeam'*
㊵ 3 × Iris *'Sam Carne'*
㊶ 2 × *'Comte de Chambord'*
㊷ 2 × Tanacetum parthenium aureum
㊸ 2 × Geranium × oxonianum
㊹ 2 × *'Buff Beauty'*
㊺ 3 × Astrantia major *'Sunningdale'*
㊻ 2 × Campanala lactiflora *'Loddon Anna'*
㊼ 2 × *'Old Blush China'*
㊽ Rosmarinus officinalis
㊾ 2 × *'Félicité Parmentier'*
㊿ 2 × Iris *'Beverly Sills'*
(51) 3 × Geranium nodosum
(52) 2 × *'Alfred de Dalmas'*
(53) 2 × Ruta graveolens
(54) Taxus baccata *(yew hedge surround with 4 arched entrances and 10 arched windows cut into it)*
(55) *Gravel path*
(56) 40 × Agapanthus praecox *'Albidus'*
(10 in each square tub)

Arbours should always be slightly secret and secluded places, suitable for contemplation – or a proposal of marriage! This shady arbour on the edge of a wood is based on a typical Gertrude Jekyll design, constructed from rustic poles and with a seat built into it. The fragrant arch created is in flower all summer, with scented roses 'Madame Isaac Pereire' and 'Céline Forestier' planted on it.

This pergola of generous proportions, 7ft (2m) high and 8ft (2.4m) across, creates a light and airy structure. Most of the uprights carry repeat-flowering roses while the cross-pieces are covered by more vigorous once-flowering Ramblers.

The metal-framed structure forming the side entrance to a house is covered in the Sempervirens rose, 'Félicité et Perpétue', which is semi-evergreen in all but the hardest winters.

This rose arbour is made from an old clinker-built boat sawn in half and set in a secluded corner of a country garden with the bows uppermost. It is clothed in scented Climbers.

planting
with Old Roses

PLANTING WITH OLD ROSES

The idea of growing roses with other plants has both practical and aesthetic roots, and has a long history. It was done in part to avoid the associated disease problems that arise with a monoculture. Different plants take and return different nutrients from and to the soil, and a mixed planting with roses not only reduces the incidence of specific replant disease (rose sickness) but also of mineral deficiencies in the soil. Growing only one species of plant in a bed will eventually produce a build-up of harmful micro-organisms. The ancient Greeks grew fields of roses for medicinal, cosmetic, religious and aesthetic reasons, and they underplanted their roses with garlic. This was said to be for improving the perfume, but in reality it had, like most myths, a more practical purpose – the improvement of the crop.

The aesthetic history of roses grown with other plants is also interesting. It must always have been done in an informal way; what housewife could resist tucking other plants round the feet of a rose? Medieval manuscripts show red and white roses surrounded by a wealth of other flowers in the gardens of European Christendom; associate planting of this kind was full of Christian symbolism. By the nineteenth century more orderly cottage gardens, as well as smaller town gardens, were showing a

(above) A harmonious planting of 'Tour de Malakoff' with geraniums and catmints (Nepeta), *which reflect the grey and purple tones in the rose.*

wealth of mixed cottage plants, but it was not until the latter part of the century that gardeners like Gertrude Jekyll started to use associations of flowering plants that were based on conscious principles of colour and form.

In the first half of the twentieth century Lawrence Johnston at Hidcote and Vita Sackville West at Sissinghurst took a rich palette of cottage plants – Old roses, herbaceous plants, wild plants, herbs, climbers, bulbs, shrubs and trees – to create considered but informal plantings that were designed to enhance the plants included in them. Among these flowers, roses remained predominant. But they were not the stiff, modern roses of the formal rose gardens of the larger Victorian or Edwardian houses, and they were rarely grown alone. Old roses were combined with foxgloves and hollyhocks, underplanted with old-fashioned pinks, mixed with herbaceous plantings, and their scent complemented by that of the surrounding herbs.

The value of growing Old roses in this way cannot be too highly emphasized. Not only will a better balance of nutrients in the soil be maintained, but when the roses are not in flower, the borders can still be full of colour and interest. When the roses are in flower, other colours can be used to match or contrast with the predominant pinks and whites of the roses; their round flowers, on rounded bushes, can be broken up by spire-flowered plants like foxgloves, delphiniums, lupins; and their perfume can be enhanced by that of old-fashioned pinks and low-growing scented shrubs as well as herbs.

The companion plants are divided into three main groups: plants which are in the same colour range as that of the roses; plants with complementary or contrasting colours (usually blues, yellows, greys and greens); and structural plants with a more vertical shape than that of the roses, with contrasting textures of foliage, or with spire-shaped flower heads, to lend a border height and interest. Other plants could also be grown for perfume, insects, culinary herbs and dried flowers.

When the borders are intended predominantly as rose borders, it is important that they look their best when the roses are out. You should ensure, therefore, that you include plants which will be performing at this time; too many dead areas will reduce the impact of the roses, and autumn, winter and spring plantings are better concentrated elsewhere in the garden.

(top left) The round flowers of 'De Meaux' are juxtaposed with taller, spire-flowered delphiniums, foxgloves and lychnis.

(top centre) The dusky purple and grey tones of 'Veilchenblau' are enhanced by blue and yellow in the surrounding planting.

(top right) 'Jenny Duval' is grown on a support, with dictamnus in the background.

In roses, the palette of colour is broken down into yellow, white, pink and purple. When choosing companion planting, you should also consider foliage, as it may be possible to bring interesting foliage texture to the colour group. Bear in mind the colour of the rose's stamens too: it is often feasible to pick this up in the planting partners.

COLOUR CONSIDERATIONS

If the rose border does include plants that will not be flowering at the same time as the roses, their colour, of course, does not have to be considered in relation to that of the roses. But in all other cases it does. You may choose to have a border concentrating predominantly on one colour – red, purple, white, yellow or pink – or to have a border of mixed colours. In a mixed border it is important that any colour changes happen slowly and deliberately, in drifts, so that the statements are emphatic and you avoid a piecemeal effect, what I call the "fruit salad" effect, that can be caused by too rapid jumps from one colour to another.

The idea behind companion planting is to find herbaceous plants, shrubs and herbs that pick up the colour of the rose and enhance it. In each colour group there is a huge range of plants, and what you use is largely a matter of personal choice, though there are some further considerations that will also need to be taken into account; colour is not the only criterion when working out a planting scheme. Height, foliage, texture and perfume are all important, and while plants used at the front of the border should be of a size to hide any of the rose's bare stems, those at the back or centre of the bed should provide some structural value. Flower size is important too: as a general guide, the flowers of companion plants should be smaller than those of the surrounding roses. You may also need to consider whether your proposed companion plants are invasive and whether they require staking.

The flowers of Old roses are seldom one colour, but made up of many subtle colours. One of the finest examples of this is the Gallica 'Jenny Duval'. Here the flowers are shades of grey, pink, violet and purple. And 'Ballerina' has flowers that are white-centred, with pink outer petals.

The photograph above shows how flower shape, colour and movement can extend the interest in the garden. There are four main colour groups: white, yellow, pink and purple. Red, except for the darker shades, has been excluded, as has orange, except for the pale burnt

(above) The pink and white of 'Ballerina' are picked up in the pink lamium and the white lychnis.

(above) 'Cardinal Richelieu' and a rich-flowered verbascum offer different and complementary shades of purple.

(top right) 'Celestial' with violas.

(right) In a classic partnership, the strong crimson pink of R. gallica *var.* officinalis *is seen with blue-purple catmint (*Nepeta 'Six Hills Giant').

orange, and blue; any bright, strongly coloured plants would destroy the subtlety of this kind of grouping.

HARMONIOUS COLOURS

The four colour drifts described below could be used on their own or together. If they are used together, each should be firmly established, and strong structural planting used to link them.

A PURPLE DRIFT
A small drift of purple can be achieved as shown in the photograph above right, by combining 'Cardinal de Richelieu' with a purple-flowered verbascum. Other roses of similar colouring – including 'De Rescht',

R. gallica var. *officinalis*, 'Charles de Mills' and 'Tuscany Superb' – all have tints and hues that would be enhanced by purple-shaded companion plants, such as the examples given below:

Dianthus deltoïdes
A tiny, low-growing and spreading dianthus with masses of leaves. The small flowers are a vivid purple-magenta colour. It can be grown at the base of a rose of this colour.

Viola riviniana 'PURPUREA' (V. labradorica)
This perennial viola has purple-green leaves and grows happily in the shade under roses. It flowers in early spring, before the roses, but it is the foliage that adds to the planting.

Lychnis coronaria
This herbaceous plant grows to medium height and is perfect for planting immediately next to a rose. Its tiny flowers of a brilliant shade of cerise-purple will link dianthus and rose together, and its grey, downy foliage sets off the colour of their flowers.

Cotinus coggygria
This handsome shrub is usually found growing to a height of 10ft (3m) or more, but by pruning it you can keep it to the same height as the rose, about 4ft (1.2m). Pruning also increases the size of the neat, purple leaves. The texture of the foliage gives interest to a planting, and would also make a good foil to a yellow planting beyond.

Drifting 'Daybreak' with yellow lupins.

'Buff Beauty' with harmonious yellows.

'Belle Amour' with foxgloves and geraniums.

A YELLOW DRIFT

Yellow is a difficult colour. There is a marvellous range of yellow Climbers, but very few yellows among Shrub roses. Most modern yellow roses are chrome in colour, without shading, and their habit and growth is inappropriate for mixed plantings.

The rose 'Buff Beauty' has quite strong yellow buds which rapidly fade through pale yellow to cream. Neatly pruned, it can be kept down to 4ft (1.2m).

Tanacetum parthenium aureum
This bright, golden-yellow feverfew is lovely with roses, provided you do not let it seed itself everywhere.

Meconopsis cambrica
This pale yellow Welsh poppy grows happily underneath and at the front of a rose. The short-lived single flowers and the soft foliage lends freshness to a planting.

Achillea 'MOONSHINE'
A pale yellow achillea with flat, architectural heads. The feathery grey foliage softens the surrounding green.

Hemerocallis lilioasphodelus (H. flava)
An old-fashioned day lily with scented flowers. The pointed foliage and trumpet-shaped flowers provide a pleasing contrast to rose blooms.

A PINK DRIFT

Some pink roses have a yellow tinge at the base, such as 'Mevrouw Natalie Nypels' while others, like 'Old Blush China', tend towards the blue shades.

Calamintha grandiflora
This dainty plant has small flowers held on delicate stems and aromatic foliage.

Penstemon 'APPLE BLOSSOM'
Although penstemons are not completely hardy they are delightful subjects with pretty, spire-shaped snapdragon type flowers.

Alstroemeria Ligtu hybrid
The pink, star-shaped, lily-like flowers of this perennial give delicacy to the back of a rose planting.

Geranium sanguineum VAR. striatum
A herbaceous geranium with small pale pink flowers which manages to grow up through a rose without swamping it.

Cupped 'Comte de Chambord' with geranium.

'Lavender Lassie' with white-veined pink lamium.

'Penelope' and golden feverfew.

Tall alliums lend contrast to 'Yvonne Rabier'.

A WHITE DRIFT

Use the nuances in white roses: some roses are pink in bud, while 'Yvonne Rabier' has clusters of white flowers with a mere hint of yellow at the base.

Dianthus 'MRS SINKIINS'
This reliable old-fashioned pink has frilled white flowers with the most intense perfume and pale grey foliage.

Lychnis coronaria 'ALBA'
This variety has grey foliage but an abundance of white flowers.

Philadelphus 'BELLE ETOILE'
Kept tightly pruned, this shrub will grow no more than 4ft (1.2m). The white flowers have an intoxicating perfume.

Digitalis purpurea 'ALBA'
The spire-shaped flower heads of white foxgloves lend height and architectural interest to a drift.

Lychnis coronaria *'Alba' with white flowers and grey foliage is effective seen against 'Yvonne Rabier'.*

STRUCTURAL PLANTS

Shrub roses tend to present themselves as round plants with round flowers. The use of 'structural' plants will relieve the uniformity, bringing a variety of height and form to the border, and providing useful links for different colour groupings. Here, the eye is the most critical judge of the design and the planting. Structural plants can make or break a border, and since plants (unlike furniture and paintings in a room) grow, change and die, if they turn out to be in the wrong place, they should be moved without hesitation in the autumn or, more ruthlessly, removed altogether. You must harden your heart to self-seeded foxgloves or tiny alchemilla plants which appear where you do not want them, and take notes in mid-summer to help you remember where those plants that are to be moved should ideally be placed.

Iris, hemerocallis, alliums, crocosmias, lilies, woody salvias, artemisias and summer-flowering bulbs can all be used as structural plants. They are at their best when planted as interruptions or transitions between colour groupings, and should be used sparingly and preferably in clumps. Iris are useful for creating a 'bay' in a border, which can constructively challenge the conventional planting of small, medium and large plants in layers from front to back. The object is to make a definite but subtle statement and to remember that a natural look is more desirable than a contrived one.

Plants with spire-shaped flower heads are extremely valuable used in this way: for example, foxgloves, herbaceous salvias, verbascums, campanulas, delphiniums, purple loosestrife and lupins. Some of the lower-growing verbascums and salvias can be used at the front of the border, and the taller, more stately plants in the middle or at the back. However, it is important to get the proportions right, and you should avoid choosing a variety that is so tall that it either dwarfs or obscures the surrounding planting.

(above) Foxgloves, seen here planted with 'Celestial', give height and architectural interest to the border with their elegant spires.

(top) Dwarf cotton lavender (Santolina chamaecyparissus 'Nana') delicately frames the shrub rose 'Charles de Mills'.

THE MIXED BORDER

In a mixed border it is important to provide colours that complement those of the roses. Blues and pale yellows will offset the paler pastel pinks and whites to their advantage (though use them sparingly, since too much, especially of blue, can quickly dominate a planting); silvers and purples will enhance the stronger pinks and dark red. Foliage plants or other structural plants are helpful in making the transition between drifts of strongly contrasting colours. But there are no hard and fast rules here; experimentation, and having the courage to move mistakes, is the best policy.

Here are some suggestions for plants that can be used to link the plants in the four colour drifts listed above:

Artemisia 'POWIS CASTLE'
A delightful grey feathery-leaved plant with aromatic foliage. It grows quite tall, and makes an interesting transition between pink and white. It can also be used to great effect with purple.

(above) Tall delphiniums give a cool backdrop to the white of 'Madame Hardy' in a mixed border.

(top) The spires of delphiniums, seen in this border with 'Léontine Gervaise', are echoed on a lower-growing scale by the sisyrinchium planted underneath, with 'Rosa Mundi'.

(above) Blue is effectively used to offset the pastel pink of 'Fantin Latour'.

(top) A mixed border of roses and herbaceous plants, including geraniums, white lupins, sisyrinchiums and lychnis, has a marvellous structural quality. The rose in the foreground is 'Comte de Chambord'.

'Souvenir de la Malmaison' backed by campanula.

'Complicata' with campanula and geranium.

'De Meaux' with the feathery, delicate appearance of dropwort (Filipendula vulgaris).

Nepeta 'SIX HILLS GIANT'

A large, handsome catmint with strongly scented foliage and spire-shaped, dark blue flower heads which are popular with the bees. A useful association for pinks and whites. Regular deadheading will ensure a continuity of flowers.

Campanula lactiflora 'PRICHARD'S VARIETY'

A magnificent plant growing to 5ft (1.5m). Delicate sprays of pale blue flowers are held on strong stems covered with pale green leaves. It will have a strong effect on the whole border, not just on the surrounding plants.

Delphinium 'BLACK KNIGHT'

Delphiniums have a powerful structural presence and always work well with roses. The dark purple will help to brighten up the border. Cut them down hard immediately after flowering and they will flower again in the autumn.

Rosemary and 'Old Blush China'.

'Comte de Chambord' with golden feverfew.

HERBS WITH ROSES

There is a sympathetic magic about herbs, and the value of planting them with roses cannot be over-emphasized. The subtlety and texture of the aromatic foliage tends to refine the exuberance of both roses and herbaceous flowers in a border. An area of sage always seems to provide tranquillity.

With the exception of rosemary, fennel, sweet cicely and a few others, herbs tend to be low-growing, and they are useful in creating an undulating effect in the planting. They are usually quite tolerant of shade and the majority do not mind the proximity of taller plants. Indeed, strong sunlight can brown the young growth of the golden marjoram. This herb makes a good companion for *R. gallica* var. *officinalis*, picking up the colour of the golden stamens on the rose. The thymes prefer warmth and sunlight.

The list of companionable herbs should not be restricted to culinary varieties. Rue looks wonderful with roses, although

'Madame Plantier' with the frilly foliage of parsley.

some people may be allergic to the sap and should protect their skin, especially in full sun. All the artemisias are excellent, but *Helichrysum italicum*, which has a strong curry-like aroma, should be avoided near roses. Invasive herbs like mint and lemon balm are also unsuitable,

'Reines de Violettes' with purple sage.

unless they are grown in containers.

Herbs should be cut back in late summer or mid-spring, and a failure to do this will result in bare centres, rather like a monk's tonsure. A gentle clipping of the previous season's growth will usually be sufficient.

ANNUALS IN THE BORDER

The moment the word annuals is used it tends to conjure visions of bedding plants: regimented rows of zinnias and salvias. There is prejudice against using annuals, but if carefully chosen they can lighten and adorn the border from mid- to late summer, when the once-flowering roses and most herbaceous plants are over, and the repeat-flowering roses are gathering energy for their early autumn flowering. This was clearly understood by Victorian gardeners, and the old varieties that they used, like clary (*Salvia viridis*) and the annual gypsophila, work particularly well with roses.

There is no need for greenhouses or cold frames to grow annuals. Simply sow the seeds into the soil according to the instructions on the packet, and rotate varieties to avoid poor germination in subsequent years. Small gaps and bays left for annuals in key positions in the border will yield rich rewards.

Here are some other annuals that go well with roses: *Brachycome iberidifolia* (Swan River daisy), with masses of daisy-like flowers; cornflower (*Centaurea cyanus*), with bright blue double flowers held on tall stems; *Cosmea bipinnatus*, with pale pink centres fading to white; *Lavatera* 'Pink Beauty' or *L.* 'Mont Blanc', the annual mallow; *Limnanthes douglasii*,

yellow and white flowers for a yellow drift; *Nicotiana*, the night-scented tobacco plant: *N. alata* 'Lime Green' for a yellow drift or the taller *N. langsdorffii* for the back of a border; *Matthiola bicornis*, pale pink and white night-scented stock; *Salvia farinacea* 'Victoria', with spires of violet-blue flowers; *Pyrethrum ptarmicaeflorum*, with fine silver foliage. And do not forget that odd corners in a border are the ideal places to grow annual herbs such as parsley and basil.

(above) Annuals give colour and interest to the border in mid- to late summer. Clary (Salvia viridis) is seen here with 'Felicia': its muted shades of pink, grey and purple will show up well from a distance.

(above) The purple in the bud of Belgian honeysuckle looks effective against 'Bleu Magenta'.

(left) Everlasting sweet peas (Lathyrus) grow with 'Madame Isaac Pereire', grown here as a Climber.

CLIMBING COMPANIONS

Some brilliant plant associations can be achieved with Climbing roses, though care needs to be taken over the selection of varieties and their pruning requirements. For example, honeysuckle can be used with roses on arches, and pruned hard with shears in the autumn. But it is also essential that any non-flowering growth is cut off just before the plants flower, for this growth will, if left, bind round the rose stem with fatal results.

WISTERIA
Wisterias are probably best used with roses on a pergola, and kept on separate posts. They are vigorous and should be

used only if their pruning is clearly understood. Prune wisterias like apple trees, removing all the pointed buds in early spring, and leaving the round ones to produce flowers. At the end of the summer, cut off all the long non-flowering tendrils.

EVERLASTING PEA (Lathyrus)

These can be particularly useful for providing colour in late summer. They will produce a substantial number of shoots, and these should be thinned out to leave only four or five, to prevent the lower growth on the rose from being strangled.

JASMINE

Except for *Jasminum stephanense*, these climbers are too vigorous to plant with roses. *J. stephanense* would be a good choice to grow with an old Rambler with bare stems at the bottom. It should be pruned down to the same height, approximately 6ft (1.8m), every spring, to prevent it becoming too rampant.

PASSION FLOWER (Passiflora)

Given a warm, sunny position, these climbing plants work very well with roses, especially with white varieties. The blue passion flower *P. caerulea* is the hardiest, and needs to be pruned back to 6ft (1.8m) each year in early spring.

CLARET VINE (Vitis vinifera 'PURPUREA')

The leaves of this grapevine turn a rich claret colour towards the end of the summer. It is a wonderful subject to use with roses such as 'Madame Isaac Pereire' or, for contrast, with roses like 'Sombreuil'. Vines need regular pruning to keep them neat, and it is only the mature foliage that gives the rich colour. When the flowers appear near the base of the young shoots in high summer, prune the shoots back to the

The pear and morello cherries are linked by later-flowering 'Mermaid' to provide continued interest.

White Rambler with Euonymus fortunei *'Green 'n Gold'.*

'Sombreuil' with claret vine (Vitis vinifera *'Purpurea').*

flowers; do this throughout the summer when the vine looks untidy. This will expose the tiny bitter-sweet ornamental grapes as they ripen. Once the leaves fall, snip the shoots back to old wood.

SOLANUM

With its delightful lilac flowers, *Solanum cripsum* 'Glasnevin' creates an attractive contrast with pink roses like 'Blairii Number Two' or 'Madame Caroline Testout'. The white *S. jasminoïdes* 'Album' is slightly tender but looks delightful with white roses. Solanum will grow to 20ft (6m) and needs a firm hand, as well as regular thinning out, to keep it in check. Caution: bear in mind that solanum berries are poisonous.

Roses with Clematis *'Nelly Moser'.*

CLEMATIS WITH ROSES

There are many delightful ways to use clematis with roses: to complement or contrast with Climbing roses when both plants are in flower; to flower later in the summer when once-flowering roses are over; or to grow among Shrub roses in the border.

The following rose and clematis combinations are repeat-flowering and will provide colour and interest right through the summer. This sort of planting is very effective on a pergola, providing the planting is equal and opposite on the posts (see page 16). Pruning for both climbing plants is carried out in the spring. First cut the clematis down to 3ft (90cm) and then prune the roses as outlined in the section on pruning climbing roses (see page 113).

White Climbing rose 'Sombreuil' with purple clematis 'The President'. Dark red Climbing rose 'Guinée', with white clematis 'Marie Boisselot'. Apricot-yellow Climbing rose 'Lady Hillingdon'

'Zéphirine Drouhin' and Clematis *'Star of India' are trained together through trellis.*

with the violet-blue clematis 'Vyvyan Pennell'. Pink Climbing rose 'Madame Caroline Testout' with pale blue clematis 'Perle d'Azur'.

Once-flowering Shrub roses can have their summer season extended by growing them with *Clematis* Viticella hybrids such as 'Abundance', with small rose-red flowers; 'Purpurea Plena Elegans',

with the violet-purple rosettes; and 'Kermesina' (Viticella Rubra), with small wine-red flowers. All these clematis are pruned in early spring.

There are some fascinating species of clematis that can be used effectively with Ramblers, but since these require little or no pruning and can look untidy during the winter, it is better to use them where

'Blush Noisette' with Clematis 'Hagley Hybrid'.

the Ramblers are grown through trees rather than in the formal garden. The winter- and early spring-flowering varieties are: *C. armandii* and its cultivars, *C. alpina* and its cultivars, *C. macropetala* and its cultivars, and *C. cirrhosa* var. *balearica*. Autumn-flowering varieties include *C. flammula*, with creamy, fragrant flowers, and *C. flammula* 'Rubra Marginata', white with ruby edges, both of which have small flowers, quite reminiscent of Rambling roses.

Always avoid *C. montana*, which is too vigorous to be grown with roses, and use *C. tangutica* with a Rambler only if it is cut back to 6ft (1.2m) in early spring.

Some of the smaller clematis can be used in the border to grow over and among Shrub roses. The roots of the clematis can be enclosed in old land drains to provide shade and moisture and to prevent damage from careless hoeing. The Viticellas are the best to use for this purpose, and go well with once-flowering Shrub roses, especially the Albas. The larger hybrid clematis can provoke an identity crisis, with their huge flowers and too much foliage obscuring the flowers of the roses.

Clematis 'Recta' is seen growing through the Shrub rose, R. gallica *var.* officinalis.

CLIMBING ANNUALS WITH ROSES

The use of climbing annuals with roses is in the best traditions of the cottage garden. The nasturtium 'Peach Melba', as well as fragrant sweet peas, the edible purple-podded pea, and canary creeper can all be used as delightful and amusing companions. Annuals used like this should be planted in rotation on the opposite side of the rose each year.

PERFUMED COMPANIONS

For most of us the perfume of plants is one of the most enjoyable aspects of gardening. One of the pleasures of visiting the great flower shows is the competing perfumes of roses, hyacinths, narcissi and pinks, all out of season and vying with each other for our attention. There are two distinct ways of bringing per-fume into the garden: by the scent of the flowers or by that of their foliage.

Most roses close up for the night, so do not give out their perfume in the evening. The eglantines (*R. eglanteria*) and *R. primula*, however, all give out the most delightful perfume on warm and humid summer evenings. This can be further enhanced by a surrounding planting of night-scented stocks and nicotianas, as well as by summer jasmine.

PLANTS TO AVOID WITH ROSES

Always beware of invasive plants. Although roses are deep-rooted, they resent any plant so invasive that it will deprive them of moisture and nutrients. Lilies-of-the-valley, bluebells, ivies and Solomon's seal (*Polygonum*), as well as a number of clump-forming herbaceous plants, are among the list of undesirables. Since nurserymen and garden

'Buff Beauty' enhanced by English honeysuckle.

Lavender can be grown for perfume and texture.

centres are sometimes spare with their information on the ability of a plant to spread, and because different soil types can make a huge difference to a plant's vigour, if in doubt, weed it out.

Avoid, too, plants whose scent competes unfavourably with that of the roses. The curry plant (*Helichrysum italicum*) is a prime example. And always avoid plants with flowers that are larger and beefier than the rose they accompany. Some peonies come into this category, and some of the more voluptuous, large-flowered hybrid clematis can outshine their neighbours.

(above) The climbing hydrangea (H. petiolaris), with its creamy-white panicles of flowers, is complemented by the white blooms of Rambling roses, making an ideal partnership for a north-facing wall.

directory
of Old
Roses

DIRECTORY OF OLD ROSES

INTRODUCTION TO THE DIRECTORY

There are over 2,000 varieties of old-fashioned roses still grown commercially and in private collections. The differences between many of them are so marginal that even experts can disagree. In drawing up a list of 140 varieties it is inevitable that there will be criticism of those included or excluded. The criteria I have used are: availability, reliability and disease resistance. For example, there are at least twenty white-flowered Ramblers, all very similar, and choosing between them is an entirely subjective matter. I have, however, included some roses that have been raised by hybridizing with old varieties. The repeat-flowering Ramblers, for example,

fill a gap in the range, and, although modern in introduction, they are nevertheless 'old' in habit, justifying their inclusion.

In Flemish and Dutch still life paintings the beauty of the flowers can be seen in every detail, but they appear in isolation. What cannot be seen is the size of the flower in relation to the shrub, its foliage and its general habit. This tradition continues in modern rose catalogues, with their often very beautiful photographic flower portraits which nevertheless tell only part of the story. Beautiful as the blooms of the older varieties of rose are, it is the performance of the plant in the garden

that interests me here, and not of the flower for the exhibition vase. So my aim has been to provide a balanced collection that will enable gardeners to choose the right rose for a particular position — an essential element in designing and planting with roses.

The heights and widths given for each rose show the size that it will achieve when established and in flower. This is important when you are planning your garden; the appearance of a young plant can be extremely deceptive, and it is easy to end up with a congested border. However, climate, soil type and pruning also make a considerable difference to the ultimate size of any plant.

'JENNY DUVAL'

PERFUME IN ROSES

Just as the colours of Old roses are made up of many subtle shades, so are the perfumes. The combination of the different elements is part of the joy. The Victorians were very keen on roses, and there is a portrait of Queen Victoria with two roses, 'Niphetos', a white Tea, and 'Maréchal Niel', a yellow Tea, lying on her desk. The roses were not put in water, and as they started to die, the scent became more intense.

The favourite of Victorian gardeners were the Moss roses. The calyx and flower stalks are covered in soft spines which are scented with a rich balsam fragrance. A cut rose twirled through the

'LORD PENZANCE'

fingers releases the balsam fragrance, which combines delightfully with the rose's own perfume.

Most of the Gallicas, Centifolias, Damasks and Mosses have this balsam scent in the leaves. On a warm, humid day there is an elusive

'BELLE AMOUR'

perfume throughout the garden. Another bonus is that deer and rabbits find these less palatable than China roses.

Musk rose perfume is found in 'Rambling Rector' and in *R. moschata*, its autumn-flowering sport. We have a 'Rambling Rector', growing in a willow tree, that picks up the prevailing wind and perfumes the whole garden with its pungent and gingery scent. The Noisette roses carry this scent in combination with the scent of Tea roses, and it is particularly good in 'Noisette Carnée' where it comes over with a hint of cloves. The Hybrid Musks are quite sweet-scented, and the musk perfume is less noticeable. 'Lady Hillingdon' is one of the finest examples of the Tea perfume. The delightful bitter-sweet note appears again in the climbing Bourbons: 'Gloire de Dijon' is an excellent example.

It does seem that most classes of rose have a recessive gene in perfume that occurs as the myrrh scent. The best example of this is found in the Damask × Alba hybrid 'Belle Amour'. This rose has unknown origins but it is assumed to have some Damask parentage. The myrrh scent is quite exotic and not at all what you would expect from a rose.

The most scented leaves are provided by the eglantines with their apple-scented foliage. The scent is at its best on a hot mid-summer's day or in the evening after a shower. The smaller, double form hybrid Sweet Briar, 'Manning's Blush', is the best garden variety to plant near a seat or anywhere you pass frequently. The larger 'Lord Penzance' can be grown on a wall, and, with *R. primula*, is the ideal rose to grow as a column between two windows.

The conclusion of all this is to grow companion plants

'RAMBLING RECTOR'

with differing perfumes to enhance that of the roses. This is discussed in detail in the chapter on companion planting, Planting with Old Roses (see page 47).

It is often said that modern roses have lost their perfume. This is generally true, and in the case of florists' cut roses it is indeed deliberate. Cut roses are now grown and airfreighted all over the world, and they need to have a long life in the bud stage. It was found that perfume acted as a stimulus to open the buds, and it was therefore purposely bred out.

Rose picking in Isparta, Turkey, where the roses are grown in small plots known as 'rose gardens'

ROSES FOR PERFUMERY AND COSMETICS

The manufacture of attar of roses (the essential rose oil) makes fascinating reading. Rose oil is one of the most expensive essential oils to be used in cosmetics, and costs today between £2,500 and £3,000 a litre. A litre represents some 3 tonnes of fresh petals, 18 tonnes of boiling water, and involves 100 people picking the flowers between dawn and 10 o'clock in the morning.

Two different types of rose are used: the Damask rose 'Kazanlik' ('Trigintipetala', 'Milleri', 'Professeur Émile Perrot') is the rose grown in Bulgaria, Turkey and Iran for these essential oils, and was named after Kazanlûk, the principal town in Bulgaria, in The Valley of the Roses. The valley is about 30 miles (48km) wide and 50 miles (80km) long. On either side are mountain ranges. It is a magical place, with pure light and pure water from the mountains. In early June the wild flowers make a rich carpet and enormous, straight walnut trees testify to the lack of pollution.

The rose fields are vast, and the roses stay productive for twenty years. They are planted in wide rows and receive little or no care in terms of pruning or spraying. Weeding between the plants is unnecessary because of their size, and weeding between the rows is done by tractor or rotovator. This entirely organic form of cultivation, taken together with the local microclimate and water from the mountains, all contribute to the purity of the final product.

The maximum altitude for growing roses was always considered to be between about 4,000 and 6,000ft (1,200–1,800m), but a farm in Iran has recently pioneered growing roses at 10,000ft (3,000m). Because of the lower boiling point of water at this altitude and the purity of light, the rose oil that they produce is probably the finest in the world.

(above) R. 'Kazanlik' is still used to make rose water.

(left) In this ancient still, the rose petals are boiled for 3–4 hours and the resulting oil is collected. The water is then boiled for a second time.

(above right) The slurry of boiled rose petals is sun-dried to provide winter fuel.

(right) Rose water for sale.

The 'Bulgaria Rose' factory in Kazanlûk is the most advanced of its kind, and to stand over a tonne of roses while the still is being loaded is literally intoxicating. The roses are boiled for about four hours, and a small amount of oil collected in the condenser. The water is boiled a second time, to separate out any remaining rose oil, and then sold as rose water. If, however, the water is only boiled once, and the oils retained in it (requiring less sophisticated equipment), the resulting rose water has remarkable properties, like the regeneration of facial tissue.

Rose perfume is made from *R. × centifolia*, the cabbage rose, grown in Morocco and around Grasse in the South of France. It cannot be distilled in the traditional way, because it has a very low yield when hydrodistilled, and the method used is to steep the petals in wax which, when drawn off, leaves a residue known as 'concrete'. Hexane is then used to dissolve out the fragrant oils from the 'concrete'. Today, blended flower perfumes have overtaken unadulterated rose perfume, and the chemicals that give the violet its scent are often used to enhance the scent of the rose.

The oil produced in this way cannot be used in an atomizer and is limited to use in cosmetics and what my Grandmother used to call handkerchief perfume. 'Kazanlik' perfume has a lemony overlay, very different from that of the rose perfume made from *R. × centifolia*, which is rich and sweet.

When over-production caused a slump in Pakistan's pot-pourri industry, they decided to see whether it was possible to use the Floribunda roses they were growing for the production of rose water. The plan failed because the modern repeat-flowering roses are descended from China roses, and derive their perfume from *R. × chinensis* ('Hume's Blush Tea-scented China'), whose scent is like that of freshly harvested tea. It is not possible to use this in a perfumer's formula, since it has a bitter note that cannot be easily detected in the flowers.

JAM FROM ROSES

Rose petal jam has long been considered a great delicacy, from the beginnings of cooking. Even as early as Elizabethan times in England, cookery books stressed the need for using Damask roses.

In the hills of Isparta, in Turkey, the roses for jam are picked along with the roses for perfume, from the fields known as 'rose gardens'. The rose used is the Damask rose, 'Kazanlik' ('Trigintipetala', 'Milleri', 'Professeur Émile Perrot'). As with roses for perfume, no other class of rose can quite equal the flavour of the Damasks (although you can use 'Comte de Chambord' and 'Rose de Rescht' successfully for jam-making).

Whereas whole rose flowers are used for making perfume, the petals have to be separated from the flower heads for jam, in order to remove the bitter note from them. The stamens are also removed and thrown away. Ancient recipes also called for the removal of the yellow base of each petal, to improve the colour and the sweetness of the rose petal jam. The petals are then graded and the best kept to one side for adding to the jam at the end.

The majority of petals are thrown into sacks on the ground. As soon as they are all sorted, these petals are mixed with an equal amount of sugar and pulverized by hand, a strenuous task usually given to the young men of the village. The resultant 'mush' then goes off to a factory, where extra sugar transforms the pulp into a somewhat sickly-sweet form of jam.

(above) The petals are separated from the flowers by hand. All age groups join in this operation, under the shade of a walnut tree, as the work must be completed by lunchtime.

(right) The finest petals are selected for their colour and texture and separated out from the rest. These will be lightly steamed and added to the finished jam at the end. As soon as they are graded, they are sealed into airtight drums to prevent wilting or discoloration before the jam is made. The remaining petals are mixed with sugar and then pulverized by hand.

ROSE PETAL RECIPES

I am very grateful to John and June Morris of the Grafton Manor Hotel
for the following recipes which are based on 'Comte de Chambord', and
are easy to make in a domestic kitchen.

Rose Petal Jam

Pick the flower early in the morning before they are fully open. Remove the stems (for additional colour and sweetness, cut off the yellow base of the petals), then weigh the petals and place them in the same volume of water. Stir in a covered pan for half an hour, by which time it will have a wonderful smell but an uninteresting colour. Increase the heat and slowly add jam sugar (sugar with added pectin) weighing double the weight of the petals. The colour will change dramatically to a deep pink. Bring the mixture to the boil and keep it at a rolling boil for four minutes, by which time a drop poured onto a plate should form a skin. Pour into warm jars and allow to cool. Then place the tightly sealed jars in a dark, cool cupboard.

Rose Petal Sorbet

To make a delicious sorbet use three tablespoons of rose jam, a pint (450ml) of water and the juice of one or two lemons. Place in a sorbetière and turn to a smooth, creamy mixture. This can then be stored in a sealed plastic box in the freezer which, as June says, will enable you to taste and smell your garden in the middle of winter.

(above) Rose petal jam is delicious and easy to make.

It has been said that the rose is an index of civilization. Their origins date back at least to the time of these ancient Islamic pillars at Attabey, near Isparta, in Turkey.

HISTORY OF THE ROSE

Wild roses occur only in the northern hemisphere. They belong to the Rosaceae family, which includes fruit trees such as apples, pears, plums, and *Crataegus* (thorn).

The earliest known representation of a rose comes from a Tsudi grave in the mountains of Arctic Siberia, where silver votive medals (or possibly coins, though bearing no inscription) were found,

dating from 4000BC, engraved with an open single rose.

Tablets record that roses were grown by the Sumerians (living in Mesopotamia between the Rivers Tigris and Euphrates before 2000BC, in what is now Iraq). When King Sargon founded the city of Agade he is known to have sent there 'two species of fig trees, vines, rose trees and other plants'. The island of Crete lay on the trade routes between the Levant and

Europe, and jewellery from the Early Minoan period (c.2800–c.2400BC) includes modelled roses. The 'Blue Bird Fresco' in the palace at Knossos, which was virtually destroyed in an earthquake about 1450BC, has the earliest known painting of a rose.

From there the rose appears to have travelled to other parts of the Mediterranean. On tablets found in the palace of Nestor at Pylos in southern Greece (destroyed by fire in

the thirteenth century BC), there is mention not only of olive oil, but also of rose oil; and coins from Rhodes, dating from about 500BC, are imprinted with the rose.

The Greeks knew and loved roses. The rose was the flower of Aphrodite, goddess of love; Sappho called the rose 'the queen of flowers'. And the naturalist-philosopher Theophrastus (c.370–c.286BC), in his systematic classification of all known plants of the time, mentions a hundred-petalled rose; he distinguished the single-flowered wild dog rose (*kynosbaton*) from the double ones (*rhodon*), as well as describing their cultivation.

By the time the Roman civilization took over, roses had become an indulgence. Not only were they grown for decorative purposes (depicted on Pompeian frescoes), but garlands of roses were awarded to military heroes. Roses became a symbol of ostentatious wealth: Nero, like others but on a grander scale, spent some of his great wealth strewing his banqueting floors with rose petals, and showering them on his guests.

The rose survived the upheavals of the post-Roman period, and it was cultivated in the Byzantine Empire and in Persia. During the centuries preceding the First Crusade in 1095, there are mentions of rose gardens in Germany and France, and of roses grown in monastery gardens throughout western Europe. When the Moors from north Africa descended on southern Spain in AD 711, they filled the caliph's gardens outside Córdoba with roses as well as with other flowers.

The Crusades introduced Europe to the varieties of rose cultivated in Asia, and by the early seventeenth century a number of different species and varieties (the result of sports or natural crosses) were being described in

The rose was a potent symbol of Roman society

Stylized roses are carved into these 2,000-year-old pillars at Antioch, Turkey

printed Herbals in England and elsewhere in Europe.

European settlement of the New World introduced cultivated roses from Europe to North and South America. The Spanish took with them 'Castilian' roses, believed to be Damasks introduced by the Moors, while the English took plants of Gallicas and Albas. The settlers, in return, sent back to Europe specimens of indigenous American species: *R. virginiana* and *R. californica*.

In the meantime, China had grown roses for centuries, and had notably been cultivating the wild repeat-flowering single rose found in Ichang Province in Central China. But it was only at the end of the eighteenth century that the China rose reached the West – via Bengal. The first to arrive in Europe was the dark red, double, remontant *R. chinensis* var. *semperflorens* ('Slater's Crimson China'), which quickly transformed

European roses after its introduction in 1789.

The Empress Josephine had much to do with this. Her passion for roses seems to have begun in 1804, and she quickly filled the garden at La Malmaison with roses from French and English nurseries. André Dupont, a nurseryman and enthusiastic hybridizer, was responsible for the collection, and by the time of the Empress's death in 1814, this represented some 250 different varieties. Her knowledge and love of roses had a great influence on the appreciation and development of roses from then on. She encouraged hybridization, gathered leading botanists around her, and commissioned botanical artist Pierre-Joseph Redouté to paint her roses.

By the mid-1800s all efforts were being directed towards developing repeat-flowering roses, and by the 1890s the first Hybrid Teas had evolved. These soon influenced the way roses were grown, and the Victorian and Edwardian isolated 'rose garden' began.

Many of the older varieties were by this time in danger of disappearing, and cottage gardens became repositories for the Old roses. It was to these that Gertrude Jekyll and Vita Sackville-West turned when wishing to reintroduce Old Shrub and Climbing roses to their gardens. Today, the best forms of these Old roses are being welcomed back into gardens all over the world.

'STANWELL PERPETUAL'

INFLUENCE OF CLIMATE

One of the chief delights of growing Old roses is that they are not predictable. Each summer brings its own weather, and the roses change subtly every year. Light levels play an important part; for example, 'Stanwell Perpetual' achieves a wonderful pink colour in low lights, and 'Madame Isaac Pereire' a richer, darker colour in the lower light of early autumn.

Sometimes the gardener is rewarded with a perfect summer but so often this is not the case. Photographs of the roses in past summers are revealing, because each rose reacts individually to different conditions and the garden is never quite the same each year – indeed, this is part of the fascination and continual challenge of growing roses.

These older roses will nevertheless often thrive in difficult conditions and in places where Modern roses will not grow: the Albas in dappled shade or at bitter windswept altitudes; the Rugosas almost on the seashore; and the Gallicas on chalk, or on windswept coasts where the air is so pure that fungal diseases are rife (the sulphur that is present in polluted air tends to suppress fungal growth).

Heat can send the flowers over quickly, particularly the darker colours, and if possible roses should be planted where they receive some shade. However, heat is also a wonderful stimulus for perfume, and the speed of photosynthesis can produce more perfectly-shaped flowers than in cooler climates.

Heat of course can also give rise to thunderstorms, and a storm will not only cause the flower buds to rot, but will discourage insects and prevent pollination from taking place, leading to fewer rose hips in the autumn.

One useful way of stopping flowers from balling (going brown and rotting), is gently to remove the outer petals. This is quite effective on varieties like 'Comte de Chambord'. Some varieties that set hips, like *R. gallica officinalis* and *R. × alba* 'Alba Maxima', will 'die' badly, leaving brown petals after heavy rain or as they go over. If you rub the whole cluster gently between the palms of your hands when the petals are dry, they will fall off easily, together with any dead hips, leaving the viable hips behind. This job is done surprisingly quickly and makes quite a difference to the appearance of the shrub.

Soil fertility plays an important part in the quality of foliage and flowers, but this is especially so if climatic conditions are uncertain. Fertile soil is also crucial for the performance of repeat-flowering roses later in the summer. A little 'fine tuning' with foliar feed can help in difficult summers.

ROSE HIPS

Quite apart from their use in jams, jellies and wine, hips are wonderfully decorative in early winter. When working out a planting plan it is often worth considering a rose variety with good autumn colour in its hips. It need not be placed in a key position since it will achieve its prominence once the first frosts arrive and other plants have died down or lost their leaves.

With the exception of Rugosas, most repeat-flowering roses do not produce a profusion of hips. Regular deadheading prevents this anyway, of course, but if deadheading is stopped in late summer there should then be time for hips to develop if they are going to.

The best hips come from the once-flowering varieties. There is a doubtful hypothesis

A robin on 'WEDDING DAY'

'Frau Dagmar Hartopp'

called 'petalage' which proposes that roses of comparable vigour – one once-flowering, the other repeat-flowering – will produce the same number of flowers in a year. Given a kind summer with sufficient warmth for the bees to work, the number of hips on certain once-flowering varieties can certainly be phenomenal – an indication of the number of flowers that have been produced. It is interesting that varieties like *R. gallica* 'Versicolor' ('Rosa Mundi') and *R. gallica* var. *officinalis*, with little detectable scent, are so popular with the bees.

Late summer pruning (see page 107) is important in helping to set the size and quantity of hips.

For small gardens the best varieties of rose for hips are *R. gallica* 'Versicolor', *R. gallica* var. *officinalis*, and 'Frau Dagmar Hartopp'. Kept neatly pruned, they will grow to 3ft 6in (1m), and provide colour and interest in summer and autumn. For larger areas, the Species and their hybrids are quite spectacular; firm favourites are 'Complicata' and 'Shropshire Lass'. Intermediate roses growing to 5ft (1.5m) are *R. × alba* 'Alba Maxima', 'Belle Amour', 'Wolley-Dod' (*R. villosa* 'Duplex') and 'Roserie de l'Hay'. Most of the single-flowered Ramblers set hips, but the most spectacular is 'Wedding Day'. At Woodlands House there is one tumbling over a low wall, and at Christmas it is covered with robins and blackbirds; we also use the hips for table decorations. It is an excellent rose to plant against an old tree, where it will provide pollen for the bees, secure nesting sites for birds, and finally a food source in the winter.

R. gallica var. *officinalis*, also known as the 'Apothecary's Rose', was extensively cultivated by the monks at Provins in France, and the jelly produced from the hips was reputed to have excellent healing qualities. This was probably due to the high level of vitamin C, which would have been absent from a twelfth-century diet in winter. Rose hips were also gathered extensively during World War II for their vitamin C; the source in this instance was the wild dog rose in the hedgerows.

Hips of the wild dog rose (R. canina)

CLASSIFICATION

Part of the pleasure in growing Old roses is that the colour and shape of the flowers, as well as the foliage and habit of the plants, are all compatible. Their differences are subtle enough to be interesting without being disconcerting, and the separate classes into which these roses are divided taxonomically are really only important to the ordinary gardener for two reasons: one is pruning (the essential here is to know whether they are once-flowering or repeat-flowering, whether they are Climbers or Ramblers), and the second is cultivation (you need to know whether they are tender and require a warm wall, or whether they are shade-tolerant and hardy). There is, for example, little difference in how the once-flowering Albas and Gallicas should be treated, or how the repeat-flowering Hybrid Perpetuals and Bourbons should be pruned.

Most authorities anyway accept that the classification of roses is open to debate, and perhaps some of the elusive magic would be lost if the secrets and mysteries surrounding this romantic plant were to be unravelled. The rose has undoubtedly come a long way from its original species; even many of the species held in botanical collections are probably quite different from the original

THE GALLICAS have dark green foliage, with seven pointed leaves, and thin, hair-like thorns. They produce deep-coloured flowers in shades of red and purple.

THE DAMASKS have soft, pale green foliage, seven leaves and both hair and thorns. Their flowers have a pronounced perfume.

THE CENTIFOLIAS have matt green foliage with seven leaves, and both hair and scimitar-shaped thorns. Their flowers are in rich, warm shades of pink. They are most readily distinguished from the Damasks by their pronounced winged calyx.

MOSS ROSES have distinctive moss over the calyx, and their flowers have a balsam fragrance. Their foliage comprises seven leaves and their stems are thorny.

THE ALBAS have pale, greeny-grey foliage, with seven leaves, and pointed, scimitar-shaped thorns. Their flower colours are ideal for introducing pastel pinks and white.

THE BOURBONS have five leaves, upright growth and shark-fin shaped thorns. They flower throughout the summer.

plants. This is particularly true of Himalayan species which have a remarkable diversity in their seedlings. In their own climate, natural selection ensures some continuity of the strain, but in Europe nearly all the seedlings survive; *R. filipes*, for example, takes this continuity to the extent of producing seedlings which have reddish-brown leaves.

Hybrids are especially difficult to place in their correct group, and their origins are often a matter of informed guesswork. The convention is that the seed parent dictates the class, in spite of the fact that the rose may take after the pollen parent in habit. For example, 'Céline Forestier' is classed as a Noisette (seed parent 'Champneys' Pink Cluster') but its habit is far more like its pollen parent, an unknown yellow Tea rose.

Putting a rose into a class is the easiest way of identifying one whose name you do not know, and here the leaves and thorns will often tell you more than the flower itself. The photographs on these pages show the foliage as well as the flowers, of the various classes of rose – although using these criteria as a guide becomes slightly more confusing with hybrids. However, once the class is established, the flower colour usually gives you sufficient information to arrive at a much shorter list of possible identifications.

ONCE-FLOWERING SHRUB ROSES

'BELLE DE CRÉCY'

Almost the first question to be asked is whether a rose is once- or repeat-flowering. In a tiny garden it is of course important that as much as possible is repeat-flowering, yet many of our favourite garden plants only flower once during the summer: magnolias, viburnums, peonies, lilies, for example, and countless others. To reject a rose on the grounds that it is not repeat-flowering is to miss some of the most beautiful and refined of all garden plants.

The differences between once- and repeat-flowering Shrub roses become significant when consideration of texture and shape are important. These are often more noticeable when the garden is not in flower. For example, in early spring the dark green foliage of a Gallica like 'Charles de Mills', with its many branches, contrasts well with the pale yellow-green of 'Tour de Malakoff'. And during the winter months the neat architectural skeleton of 'Félicité Parmentier' and other Albas brings structure to the garden. However well-presented a repeat-flowering rose, it is very difficult to achieve a firm yet productive look, with the possible exceptions of the Portland Damasks. Once-flowering Shrub roses are better presented in this respect. The once-flowering roses are also considerably hardier than the repeat-flowerers. In areas with cold winters and a short summer season, it is hardly worth considering repeat-flowering roses: since the first flowering only takes place in mid- to late summer, there is no time for any extension of the season. However, the much hardier once-flowering roses do very well in this type of climate. Though the spring is late to start, the weather and the soil then warm up steadily through to the summer, with no setbacks, and the roses, when they flower, produce blooms of an excellent size and quality.

THE GALLICAS

This is one of the oldest classes of rose. R. gallica is a small, almost thornless rose species, found wild in Italy, Switzerland, Austria and France, and known to the Ancient Greeks and before them to the Persians. New Zealand archaeologists used the presence of these roses, which are not native to the southern hemisphere, to establish the sites of early immigrants. Gallicas are distinguished by handsome, usually dark green foliage, and dense, twiggy growth. They have a diversity of flower colour, especially in shades of purple and red, and they are almost indispensable in a mixed planting. Once established on their own roots they are great survivors. They require quite firm treatment (outlined in the chapter on pruning, page 106) when grown as shrubs, and many of them make excellent subjects for growing on pillars, obelisks and over arches.

At some stage in its history R. gallica produced a sport with large, striking, semi-double crimson-pink flowers. This rose found its way into a Saracen's garden and was discovered there during the Crusades. Eleanor of Aquitaine adopted it as her personal emblem, and on her marriage to Henry II of England it became the 'Red Rose of Lancaster'. R. gallica 'Versicolor' ('Rosa Mundi') is one of the oldest garden cultivars to survive today and was described in 1583 by Clusius; the rest are almost all nineteenth-century cultivars.

'BELLE DE CRÉCY'

The flowers of this rose first open a rich pink, and quickly fade to mauve and pink as the flower ages. They have a distinctive Gallica perfume. Any one of these shades can be picked out for the surrounding planting: Astrantia major 'Hadspen Blood' makes an excellent companion. Like most Gallicas, 'Belle de Crécy' is very good in the garden when grown as a Climber. Introduced by Rosier, 1820, and named after the town in France.
4ft × 3ft (120cm × 90cm).

'BELLE ISIS'

'BELLE ISIS'

This rose could easily be passed by in favour of one of its showier cousins. In this way its delicacy and refinement would be missed. The flower size, foliage and habit are nicely balanced and in keeping. The flowers are a soft pale pink with an unusual spicy fragrance, sometimes described as the scent of myrrh. An ideal subject for the front of a border. Introduced by Parmentier, Belgium, 1845.
3ft 6in × 3ft (100cm × 90cm).

'CAMAIEUX'

An unusual rose, with pale pink flowers striped with a deep crimson, although not as dramatically striped as *R. gallica* 'Versicolor' ('Rosa Mundi'). The flowers can show green centres and proliferation. It is best to leave the pruning until the last moment in mid-spring. It is an easy rose to grow and produces small, orange-yellow hips in the autumn. Introduced by Vibert, France, 1830.
4ft × 3ft (120cm × 90cm).

'GLOIRE DE FRANCE'

'CARDINAL DE RICHELIEU'

One of the darkest-flowered Gallicas, with dusky purple flowers that reflex with age. The rich hue of the purple makes it a good subject for planting with grey-leaved plants and verbascum. It makes a fine Climber, especially on a pillar. Introduced by Laffay, France, 1840.
4ft × 3ft (120cm × 90cm).

'CHARLES DE MILLS'

A striking and handsome rose with one of the most beautiful flower shapes. The petals are arranged in quarters held in a saucer shape. The flowers start crimson and fade to purple. The perfume is elusive and

'CHARLES DE MILLS'

can only be detected by some people. Origin uncertain but probably about 1850.
5ft × 4ft (1.5m × 1.2m).

'GLOIRE DE FRANCE'

In many respects this rose epitomizes the pleasure of growing the older varieties, the flowers being interesting at every stage. The buds open to a cup shape of quartered petals in a soft mauve-pink which fades to pale pink as the flowers unfold and reflex. Good rich perfume. Introduced by Rosier, France, 1820.
3ft 6in × 3ft (100cm × 90cm).

'CARDINAL DE RICHELIEU'

'L'IMPÉRATRICE JOSÉPHINE'

'LORD SCARMAN'

'LORD SCARMAN'

The flowers of this rose demonstrate one of the most attractive features of the Old rose: while the petal facing is red, the reverse of the petals is a remarkably different pale purple. This judicial mix of purple and red gives richness to the large flowers. Disease-free and vigorous, it is also a good subject for climbing on a shady wall. Raised and introduced by Scarman, UK, 1995.
5ft × 4ft (1.5m × 1.2m).

'POMPON DE BOURGOGNE'

'JENNY DUVAL'

This has the most intriguing flowers, and every one seems to be slightly different. The buds open in shades of purple and pink and progress through to pink, violet, lilac and white as they fade. The flowers are well quartered with a rich perfume. This rose can be included in a pink drift or a purple drift, and with a wide range of companion plants. Origin unknown, mid-18th century.
4ft × 3ft (120cm × 90cm).

'L'IMPÉRATRICE JOSÉPHINE'

Also known as *R. × franco-furtana*, this rose was one of the Empress Josephine's favourites. Though it was subsequently named after her, it is in fact an ancient hybrid with *R. majalis* (*R. cinnamomea*) and was recorded by Clusius in 1583. The flowers are large, clear pink, with a ruffled arrangement of petals. The buds are turban-shaped. It has attractive green-grey foliage. Europe, before 1583.
3ft 6in × 3ft (100cm × 90cm).

'POMPON DE BOURGOGNE'

Usually classed as a Centifolia, this rose (also known as *R. burgundiaca*) is more likely to be a sport from a Gallica. Found in 1664, this is a wonderful subject for the formal garden. The leaves are tiny and it makes a very effective hedge when not covered in small, claret-coloured flowers. It requires firm pruning to keep it small and neat.
3ft × 2ft (90cm × 60cm).

R. gallica VAR. *officinalis*

The 'Apothecary's Rose' was named thus because of the 'healing' qualities (probably the result of vitamin C) of the conserve made from the hips. Also called the 'Red Rose of Lancaster', the flowers are a bright crimson-red with yellow stamens. This is a bold colour which stands out in a mixed planting. Good, dark green foliage. Prior to the 12th century.
4ft × 4ft (1.2m × 1.2m).

R. gallica VAR. *officinalis*

R. gallica 'VERSICOLOR' (ROSA MUNDI')

R. gallica 'VERSICOLOR'

This rose (known also as 'Rosa Mundi') was supposedly named after Fair Rosamund, mistress of Henry II of England. Unfortunately, Rosamund lived many years before 'Rosa Mundi', a sport of *R. gallica* var. *officinalis*, was discovered. It is far more striking than 'Camaïeux', with pale blush-pink flowers with purplish stripes overlaid. Used in a mixed planting it is a perfect foil against pale colours. A nearly scentless rose, it is surprisingly popular with the bees which, in autumn, leave behind a legacy of pale orange hips. Origin uncertain but probably found during the 16th century.
4ft s 4ft (1.2m × 1.2m).

'TERESA SCARMAN'

This newly introduced rose shows one of the unusual traits of some Gallicas in that they darken as they fade. The flowers are a pale pink with deeper centres and as they open and reflex they darken to a reddish purple-pink. It has a strong, rich fragrance. Discovered as a seedling by Baden Fergusson. To be introduced by Scarman, UK, 1996.
4ft s 3ft 6in (1.2m × 1m).

'TUSCANY SUPERB'

This is a sport from 'Tuscany', the 'Old Velvet Rose' mentioned by Gerard in his Herbal in 1597. It has strong growth that lends itself to being planted as a Climber. The flowers are a rich dark red and suggest Gallica parentage. It produces good, dark hips in the autumn. Introduced by Paul, UK, before 1848.
5ft s 5ft (1.5m × 1.5m).

'TUSCANY SUPERB'

'TERESA SCARMAN'

'BLANCHEFLEUR'

'DE MEAUX'

THE CENTIFOLIAS

The origins of this class are uncertain, and may go back well before the date of 1600 which is given for the first raising. The flowers are double and richly scented. These are roses that thrive in hot conditions. In milder and wetter conditions the blooms are prone to rain damage, and disease may become a problem. In these conditions, 'Fantin-Latour' and 'Blanchefleur' will prove to be the best choices.

'BLANCHEFLEUR'

Easily recognized from the still life paintings of Flemish Masters. The medium-sized full flowers are white, tinged with blush. The perfume is a delight, with the full richness of this class. It comes into flower early and with

R. × centifolia

profusion. Introduced by Vibert, France, 1835.
4ft × 3ft (120cm × 90cm).

R. × centifolia

This is the rose that was grown around Grasse in the South of France for extraction of perfume. The flowers are cupped, full-petalled and charming. It is better suited to the South of France than the damp and uncertainty of more temperate summers.
Europe, before 1600.
5ft × 4ft (1.5m × 1.2m).

'CHAPEAU DE NAPOLÉON'

This rose (also known as *R. × centifolia* 'Cristata') is a sport from *R. × centifolia* with the same flowers but slightly thornier growth. The unusual shaped buds have an enlarged calyx which is covered in soft green spines with a strong fragrance of balsam. The shape of the bud gave rise to its name. It is from this development that one can see how Old Pink Moss (*R. × centifolia* 'Muscosa') sported. Discovered on a convent wall in Fribourg, Switzerland. Introduced by Vibert, France, 1827.
5ft × 4ft (1.5m × 1.2m).

'DE MEAUX'

Just as 'Pompon de Bourgogne' is the miniature of the Gallicas, so 'De Meaux' is the miniature of the Centifolias. It makes a

'CHAPEAU DE NAPOLÉON'

delightful low hedge or group at the front of a border. The centres of the flowers are deeper pink than the outer edges. Found in Bishop de Meaux's garden, 1789, France.
3ft × 3ft (90cm × 90cm).

'Fantin-Latour'

'Fantin-Latour'

Named in honour of the painter Henri Fantin-Latour at some time in the 19th century. The raiser and date are unknown but the rose would appear to have some Alba parentage. This is one of the finest of the old roses, although it has little perfume, and is an easy rose to grow. The flowers are a fine shell-pink, with occasional deeper-coloured petals giving great depth. It has attractive green foliage. France, before 1900. 5ft × 4ft (1.5m × 1.2m).

'Tour de Malakoff'

Known as the 'Taffeta Rose', this Centifolia is often described as being suitable for growing in a trailing position. This is entirely a matter of pruning, and with good training it makes an excellent upright plant. The flowers, which are open and slightly cupped, start pink and fade through purple and crimson to lavender. It has an excellent perfume. Introduced by Soupert and Notting, Luxembourg, 1856. 5ft × 4ft (1.5m × 1.2m).

'BLANCHE MOREAU'

THE MOSSES

These originated from two different sources. The first, like Old Pink Moss (R. × centifolia *'Muscosa') from* R. × centifolia, *and the second, like 'Quatre Saisons Blanche Mousseuse', as a sport from* R. × damascena semperflorens *('Autumn Damask', 'Quatre Saisons'). It is fascinating that it not only sported moss but also changed its colour from pink to white at the same time. The Damask Mosses were fertile, and most Moss roses come from this source and carry the perfume and the vigour.*

'BLANCHE MOREAU'

The dark brown mossing and the dark green foliage make a delightful contrast against the pure white flowers. This rose has a particularly excellent perfume and habit. Some writers claim it can repeat in autumn although it unfortunately does not do so in my garden. Introduced by Moreau-Robert, France, 1880.
4ft 6in × 4ft (1.35m × 1.2m).

'GÉNÉRAL KLÉBER'

One of the finest Moss roses, with biddable, upright growth, this rose is worthy of its famous name. The large flowers start blush-pink and fade to white. Fragrant green moss and pale foliage. Introduced by Moreau-Robert, France, 1856.
4ft × 3ft 6in (1.2m × 1m).

OLD PINK MOSS

Also known as *R. × centifolia* 'Muscosa', this was the original sport from *R. × centifolia*, which first occurred in 1696. The foliage is larger and the stems thornier. It is very heavily mossed and the perfume of the flowers is best appreciated when the moss is gently squeezed. The resulting combination of rose and balsam is delightful. At its best in drier, hotter climates. France, before 1700.
5ft × 4ft (1.5m × 1.2m).

OLD PINK MOSS

'GÉNÉRAL KLÉBER'

'SOUPERT ET NOTTING'

'SOUPERT ET NOTTING'

A smaller, more compact-growing Moss. It has full flowers of a strong rose-pink with a hint of lilac. It is prone to rain damage but worth this inconvenience. Said to repeat in the autumn. Introduced by Pernet, France, 1874.
3ft 6in × 2ft 6in (100cm × 75cm).

'WILLIAM LOBB'

One of the most exceptional Old roses, with flowers of a dusky purple, which can appear blue, slate-grey or lilac, depending on the light. It requires a firm hand to keep it as a shrub. Makes an exciting contrast with 'Rosa Mundi' (*R. gallica* 'Versicolor') and a blue underplanting. Introduced by Laffay, France, 1855.
6ft × 4ft (1.8m × 1.2m).

'WILLIAM LOBB'

THE ALBAS

Albas are distinguished by pale greeny-grey foliage, upright growth, and attractive, scented flowers. The photograph of R. × alba 'Alba Maxima' (right) demonstrates the hardiness of this class. According to the farmer, the cottage on this site was pulled down over fifty years ago, and the only attention this rose gets is to be pruned once a year with the tractor hedgecutter; no spraying, watering or thinning out of dead growth, nor any fertilizer, is needed or given. It shows that the mystique of pruning roses, ingrained into us, does not apply to Old roses.

'ALBA MAXIMA'

Known variously as 'Bonnie Prince Charlie's Rose', the 'White Rose of York', or the 'Jacobite Rose', this is a fuller-flowered sport from 'Alba Semi-Plena'. The flowers open a slight blush-pink and turn to a rich white. Heavy showers may turn the petals brown. When they dry out, lightly rub the cluster

'ALBA MAXIMA'

'ALBA MAXIMA'

between the palms of the hand to help the hips form. It was extensively grown as a climber in the late Middle Ages, when it was known as the 'Great Double White'. Europe, 15th century or earlier.
6ft × 4ft (1.8m × 1.2m).

'ALBA MINIMA'

'ALBA MINIMA'

A very low-growing Alba in the same style as 'De Meaux' and 'Pompon de Bourgogne', raised from 'Lesser Maiden's Blush', which is nearly extinct due to virus. It has medium-sized, very bright pink flowers held in clusters. The foliage is unusual in that it is elongated

in the manner of some of the roses depicted by Redouté that are now sadly lost. To be introduced by Scarman, UK, 1997.
2ft × 1ft 6in (60cm × 45cm).

'BELLE AMOUR'

The origins of this rose are a mystery, but it has some Damask blood that may indicate Middle Eastern derivation. The perfume is unusual: spicy and pungent, reminiscent of myrrh. The flowers are a delicate salmon-pink and extend the range of pink shades available for complementary planting. Oval orange hips in autumn. Introduced from a convent garden in Germany, around 1950.
5ft × 4ft (1.5m × 1.2m).

'CÉLESTE'

Also known as 'Celestial', this is an old variety that was greatly appreciated in the Middle Ages for the perfection of its pointed, rose-pink buds, whose association with nipples gave rise to much ribald analogy. It is a handsome plant with grey-green foliage, and with patient pruning will grow to the size indicated.
6ft × 5ft (1.8m × 1.5m).

'FÉLICITÉ PARMENTIER'

A delicate and charming shrub suitable for the small garden. The petals are pale pink on the reverse and deeper pink inside, and the swirling arrangement in the flower gives great depth and interest. Good perfume. It has a neat habit if carefully pruned. Introduced by Parmentier, France, 1836.
3ft 6in × 3ft (100cm × 90cm).

'GREAT MAIDEN'S BLUSH'

A well formed and elegant shrub, producing semi-double flowers. In low light levels the flowers open a wonderful deep pink before fading. For this reason it is an excellent subject to grow in shade. Heavy rainfall can cause the buds to rot, and a treatment of liquid potash can help if it is applied in late spring. Introduced in Europe, 15th century.
5ft × 4ft (1.5m × 1.2m).

'MADAME PLANTIER'

An Alba hybrid which retains the pale green foliage but is

'FÉLICITÉ PARMENTIER'

nearly thornless. The richly fragrant flowers are pure white and well filled with petals. It is an excellent rose to train on a pillar, arch or other garden structure and it is hardy enough to be planted on the coldest of walls. Introduced by Plantier, France, 1835.
5ft × 4ft (1.5m × 1.2m).

'QUEEN OF DENMARK' ('KÖNIGIN VON DÄNEMARK')

This is arguably the finest of the Albas, and among the best of the Old roses. 'Queen of Denmark' was a seedling of 'Great Maiden's Blush'. The flowers show the finest quartering, with slightly differing tones of warm, rich pink. This unmistakable rose has a strong fragrance and handsome foliage in addition to its beautiful flowers. Raised by Booth, UK, 1816. Introduced in 1826.
5ft × 4ft (1.5m × 1.2m).

'MADAME PLANTIER'

'QUEEN OF DENMARK'

'ISPAHAN'

THE DAMASKS

The Damasks are among the most perfumed of the Old roses. Most of the references to roses in Ancient Rome and Ancient Greece refer to Damasks, although there is controversy as to whether or not R. × centifolia was also in existence at that time.
R. × damascena bifera ('Quatre Saisons', 'Autumn Damask'), which repeat-flowers in late summer in a good season, allowed the Roman pagan festival of Rosalia, held in May, to be repeated in September on the Isle of Samos; Virgil composed a song in its honour. Damasks are natives of arid, hot regions. In temperate climates they tend to grow vigorously, and require firm pruning.

'GLOIRE DE GUILAN'
Discovered in 1949 in a remote part of Iran. Perfect-shaped Damask flowers of a warm, clear pink with a delightful perfume. The habit is less exuberant than most in this group. It can produce the odd flower in late summer. Red hips in autumn.

Introduced by Lindsay, UK, 1949.
4ft × 4ft (1.2m × 1.2m).

'ISPAHAN'
Also known as 'Pompon des Princes', this is one of the longest-flowering of the Old roses, lasting a full six weeks. The beautifully shaped buds quickly reflex to full-petalled flowers of warm, pure pink. Strongly perfumed, this rose is magnificent as a Climber. Ancient introduction, Persia.
5ft × 4ft (1.5m × 1.2m).

'THE HON. MRS CAT'
There is probably no such thing as the perfect rose, but this is the perhaps the closest, bar one characteristic. This rose has perfection in every area except the thorns, which are awesome both in size and quantity. However, it could

'THE HON. MRS CAT'

be argued that they lend character and interest. The flowers are not too large, with a loosely quartered arrangement of petals in two distinct shades of pink. The perfume from some Alba parentage is strong and persuasive. The leaves are dark green and disease-free. Introduced by Scarman, UK, 1995.
4ft 6in × 4ft (1.35m × 1.2m).

'MADAME HARDY'
A superb white rose with flowers of a fine shape, and enhanced by a small green eye. Described once as 'green-eyed, like jealousy, envious it may be of another white Damask, 'Madame Zöetmans' who, though not of such a clear complexion, is free from ocular infirmities'. The flowers open from a slight cup to a flat, fully petalled shape. It has a haunting fragrance with a lemony overtone. This is an excellent rose to use as a Climber in difficult and shady positions in the garden. Introduced by Eugene Hardy, Luxembourg Gardens, France, 1832.
5ft × 4ft (1.5m × 1.2m).

'OMAR KHAYYAM'
Edward Fitzgerald, translator

'MADAME HARDY'

'OMAR KHAYYAM'

of the *Rubáiyát of Omar Khayyam*, gathered seeds from the poet's tomb in Nashipur. The seed was sown on Fitzgerald's tomb, giving rise to this seedling. A small shrub with pale pink, fragrant flowers. Introduced in UK, 1893.
3ft 6in × 2ft 6in
(100cm × 75cm).

R. × damascena bifera

This is the original rose from Samos (known also as 'Quatre Saisons', 'Autumn Damask') which flowers again in the autumn. Typically, it has highly scented flowers in a soft pink with a delightful, ruffled arrangement of petals. The autumn flowers are produced on the young growth that is put on in mid-summer, and this should not be pruned but only tipped and shaped architecturally during the first flowering. Its slightly untidy habit should always be borne in mind when choosing a planting position. Middle East, ancient origins.
5ft × 4ft (1.5m × 1.2m).

R. × damascena bifera

REPEAT-FLOWERING SHRUB ROSES

'SCARMAN'S CRIMSON CHINA'

content, which makes the plant prone to fungal attack. The progression through Hybrid Perpetuals to Hybrid Teas does not alter this problem, particularly with regard to blackspot. The remedies are discussed in Pests and Diseases, page 138, but you will have to allow for spraying if you plant these varieties.

THE CHINA ROSES

The Chinese national flower is the peony, and although the rose may not have enjoyed the same prestige as the peony or the chrysanthemum it is known to have been cultivated in China from very early times. A Chinese vase of the tenth century shows roses which resemble 'Old Blush China' (R. × odorata 'Pallida'). The China rose bore the precious gene for continuous flowering, and this, coupled with knowledge of artificial pollination, transformed rose breeding. At the end of the eighteenth century, when the China roses first appeared in Europe, there were some 200 varieties of known roses in existence. By 1906, the French breeder Cochet produced a

'BABY'S BLUSH'

work entitled Nomenclature de tous les noms de roses connues avec indication de leur race, année de production et synonymes, which listed 10,953 varieties.

'BABY'S BLUSH'
Miniature roses tend to be disappointing, partly because they were crossed to be miniatures of modern roses. The original dwarf sport of 'Old Blush China', probably 'Roulettii', is charming. This new variety was raised for pots or window boxes and it resembles a dwarf form of 'Noisette Carnée' ('Blush Noisette'). Pretty, shell-pink flowers with a neat, dainty appearance and a delicate, spicy fragrance are held in clusters. It is a denser and less upright plant than most miniatures. Regular deadheading will ensure a continuity of flowers. Raised and introduced by Scarman, UK, 1995.
1ft 6in × 1ft 6in (45cm × 45cm).

'HERMOSA'
The soft pink flowers are cupped and formal, with slightly hanging heads, and the shrub has a charming appearance. This wonderful example of an old-fashioned rose is ideally suited for small gardens, as it does not bush

The ability to repeat-flower comes from China roses. These were introduced into England from China at the beginning of the nineteenth century, arriving on a ship from Bengal, hence the misleading synonym, Bengal roses. A Persian, Ibn-el-Awam, writing in the twelfth century, says: 'There exists near Andalou Abou-el-Khair, the rose of the mountains, the red rose, the white rose, both double, and the China rose.' This lends some weight to the suggestion that the China rose reached Persia via the Silk Route.

With notable exceptions, particularly the Portland Damask roses, there is a price to pay for the repeat-flowering rose — susceptibility to disease. The first China shrub roses to be imported, 'Slater's Crimson China' (R. chinensis var. semperflorens) and 'Old Blush China' (R. × odorata 'Pallida'; 'Parson's Pink China'), were comparatively free from disease, but when crossed with the European roses, the gene for repeat-flowering seems to trigger some change in the leaf, perhaps wax

'HERMOSA'

'MUTABILIS'

out significantly, or to plant in a group at the front of a border. Very pretty when underplanted with violas. Introduced by Marcheseau, France, 1840.
3ft 6in × 3ft (105cm × 90cm).

'MUTABILIS'

A fascinating rose, also known as 'The Butterfly Rose'. The copper-coloured buds open to yellow flowers which change to pink and crimson as they fade. Although slightly tender, it can make a spectacular Climber on a warm, sheltered wall. It is an amusing plant to grow, and any of the flower colours can be reflected in the companion planting. China, early 19th century.
4ft × 4ft (1.2m × 1.2m) as a shrub; 10ft (3m) climbing.

'OLD BLUSH CHINA'

Also known as 'Parson's Pink China' or *R. × odorata* 'Pallida', this is reputed to be the original China rose brought to Europe. Unlike some of its progeny it is nearly disease-free, and an easy rose to grow. The dainty, informal flowers are a delightful pink with a hint of blue in the shading, and held in groups of three or four. It is an ideal rose for growing in a substantial pot. Gertrude Jekyll suggested that it should be planted in combination with rosemary. China, 1789.
3ft 6in × 3ft (105cm × 90cm).

'SCARMAN'S CRIMSON CHINA'

The flowers of this enchanting rose are an unusual shade of deep, bright crimson-pink, which dissolves delicately to a pale warm yellow at the base of the petals. The reverse of the petals is a contrasting pale pink. This combination is quite in keeping with the style of China roses and probably comes from the presence of 'Comtesse du Cayla' in the parentage. This is an ideal plant to brighten up a dull corner of your garden, where it will flower all summer long. Raised and introduced by Scarman, U.K., 1995.
2ft 6in × 2ft (75cm × 60cm).

'ALFRED DE DALMAS'

'COMTE DE CHAMBORD'

THE PORTLAND DAMASKS

The origin of the Portland rose is a mystery, but it is likely that it emerged as a hybrid of a China rose, probably 'Slater's Crimson China', and a cross between a Damask and a Gallica. The Portland roses are repeat-flowering, with many branches and excellent foliage. The perfume from their Damask parentage is outstanding. This group is virtually indispensable when making a planting plan.

'ALFRED DE DALMAS'

This rose started life under the above name in 1855, introduced by Portremer. For some reason it was reintroduced as 'Mousseline' by Moreau-Robert in 1881, under which name it is generally known today. Though usually classed as a moss, it is not in fact heavily mossed. It is an excellent rose, repeat-flowering all summer, with pale blush, sweetly fragrant flowers. Ideal for the smaller garden. Introduced by Portremer, France, 1855.
3ft 6in × 3ft (100cm × 90cm).

'COMTE DE CHAMBORD'

An American rose raised as 'Madame Boll' and sent out by Boyeau as 'Comte de Chambord' in 1859. Had the Comte possessed the same virtues as the rose he might have succeeded in his political ambitions. The flowers are a clear pink, deepening in colour toward the centre. Excellent perfume and habit. One of the first in flower, and rarely out of bloom until the first frosts. France, 1863.
3ft 6in × 3ft (100cm × 90cm).

'DE RESCHT'

The neat, medium-sized crimson flowers form an attractive pompon shape. Outstanding perfume and easy habit make it a perfect choice for the small formal garden. It is one of the best repeat-flowering roses, and free from disease. Found in northern Iran, 1949, by Nancy Lindsay.
3ft × 2ft 6in (90cm × 75cm) if well pruned.

'JACQUES CARTIER'

Also known as 'Marchesa Boccella'. There is some dispute as to whether 'Comte de Chambord' or 'Jacques Cartier' is the best of the pink Portlands, but both are sufficiently distinctive to be valuable in their own way. The buds of 'Jacques Cartier' are not so attractive as those of 'Comte de Chambord', but the flowers, which are flatter, show quartering and are less prone to damage by rain. Handsome foliage and habit. Raised by Moreau Robert, France, 1868.
4ft × 3ft (120cm × 90cm).

'THE PORTLAND ROSE'

Also known as 'Portlandica' or 'Duchess of Portland', this was named after the second Duchess of Portland before 1782. The flowers are a bright crimson-pink with semi-double petals. The amount of deadheading carried out dictates the level of repeat-flowering.
3ft 6in × 3ft (100cm × 90cm).

'DE RESCHT'

'BOULE DE NEIGE'

THE BOURBONS

These roses originated from a chance cross in 1817 between 'Old Blush China' and 'Autumn Damask' (R. × damascena semperflorens), both of which were grown as hedges on the Ile de Bourbon (now Ile de Réunion) in the Indian Ocean. Roses en route from China to Europe were rested at Réunion. The original rose was a cross between a Damask and a China. Most of this class make slender upright growth which is well suited for growing as pillars or as climbers to 10ft (3m).

The perfume, like that of most modern roses, tends to be rich and sweet without the lemon overlay that characterizes the Damasks.

'BOULE DE NEIGE'

As the name implies, the white flowers quickly reflex to produce a ball shape. They are held in groups of three or four against dark green, leathery foliage. 'Boule de Neige' grows best in part shade. Introduced by Lacharme, France, 1867.
4ft 6in × 3ft (1.35m × 90cm).

'LOUISE ODIER'

Typical cup-shaped flowers with a quartering of deep pink petals with a suspicion of lilac. Flowers throughout the summer with a warm, rich perfume. Blue or mauve underplanting highlights the colour of this rose. Introduced by Margottin, France, 1851.
5ft × 3ft (1.5m × 90cm).

'MADAME ISAAC PEREIRE'

The largest and most vigorous of the Bourbons. Deep carmine-pink flowers with well arranged petals and outstanding perfume. The flowers are quite heavy and are seen at their best when the plant is grown as a Climber. Cold springs can produce green centres to the flowers, but once the warm weather arrives this rapidly disappears. The colour is stronger in the lower light

'REINE VICTORIA'

levels of the autumn. Introduced by Garcon, France, 1881.
5ft 6in × 4ft (1.75m × 1.2m).

'REINE VICTORIA'

An attractive rose of great refinement, with delicate cup-shaped flowers of a medium size and modest pink colour. Continuously in flower, with excellent Bourbon fragrance. Prune the stems after flowering, rather than just deadheading, to keep the shrub balanced. 'Reine Victoria' and its sport 'Madame Pierre Oger' (1878) are excellent subjects for a neat appearance on obelisks. Introduced by Schwartz, France, 1872.
4ft 6in × 2ft 6in (1.35m × 75cm).

'MADAME ISAAC PEREIRE'

'MADAME PIERRE OGER'

'MADAME PIERRE OGER'

A silvery-pink sport from 'Reine Victoria' with the same cup-shaped flowers, reminiscent of a water lily. The slender, upright growth makes it an ideal subject for a pillar or to be grown as a climber. Discovered by Oger and sent out by Verdier, France, 1878.
4ft 6in × 2ft 6in (1.35m × 75cm).

'SOUVENIR DE LA MALMAISON'

'SOUVENIR DE LA MALMAISON'

In 1814 Tzar Alexander was handed a rose bloom by Josephine with the words, 'Un souvenir de La Malmaison'. The occasion was the eve of Napoleon's departure to Elba. Later, in 1843, when the Grand Duke of Russia was visiting France to plan the imperial garden, he recalled this as a suitable name for an unnamed seedling sent to La Malmaison by the rose breeder, Beluze. Large flesh-pink quartered blooms, very full, flat when opened, and with a strong perfume. Reliable and repeats well all summer. There is a climbing sport, 'Souvenir de la Malmaison Climbing'. France, 1843.
4ft × 3ft (120cm × 90cm).

'VARIEGATA DI BOLOGNA'

A striped, once-flowering Bourbon with large cupped white flowers dashed with crimson. Vita Sackville-West correctly described it as needing a cool root run. Best in partial shade or as a climber on a shady wall. Introduced by Bonfiglioli, Italy, 1909.
5ft 6in × 4ft (1.65m × 1.2m).

THE HYBRID PERPETUALS

The Chinas, Portlands, Bourbons and Noisettes all played a part in the Hybrid Perpetuals which emerged in the 1830s; they in turn, when crossed with the Tea roses, gave rise in the 1880s to Hybrid Teas. The dark reds and purple shades came from the Gallica influence, and the novelty of the colours was greeted with great enthusiasm. Although claiming to be repeat-flowering, they tend in fact to flower in two main flushes, in early summer and autumn, with occasional blooms between these times.

By 1902, some 1,700 varieties of Hybrid Perpetuals were amassed by Jules Gravereaux at La Roserie de L'Hay-les-Roses on the edge of Paris. The speed of this explosion was due to the understanding of artificial pollination, but very little attention was paid to disease or habit. Part of the difficulty of hybridizing is finding a good seed parent and, regrettably, the commercial pressure overrode considerations of disease-resistance. Goethe summed this up: 'In order to spend on one side, nature is forced to economize on the other.' Some of these 'blood lines' are still in the genetic inheritance of today's roses, which means that though their common ancestors made good seed parents, they are often susceptible to disease.

'BARON GIROD DE L'AIN'

A most attractive and unusual rose with large, dark crimson flowers with the outside edge of each petal finely etched with white. This characteristic may have come from the China Rose, 'Fabvier'. Like 'Ferdinand Pichard', 'Baron Girod de l'Ain' makes a good contrast in the border with pale pastel colours. Introduced by Reverchon, France, 1897.
4ft × 3ft (1.2m × 90cm).

'BARONNE ADOLPH DE ROTHSCHILD'

'BARON GIROD DE L'AIN'

'BARONNE ADOLPH DE ROTHSCHILD'

Also known as 'Baroness de Rothschild', this is one of the first of the 'exhibition roses'. It has very large flowers of a feminine rose-pink which deepen towards the centre. It has straight stems and makes an excellent cutting rose, although it has no perfume. It is more likely to have been the parent of 'Frau Druski' than 'Madame Caroline Testout'. Though very good in the flower border, its stems need to be hidden by lower-growing plants. Introduced by Pernet, France, 1868.
5ft 6in × 3ft (1.65m × 90cm).

'EMPEREUR DU MAROC'

Acclaimed as the darkest rose of its time. Its rich maroon petals tinged with purple are held in flat flowers which have a rich and powerful fragrance. It is a tender shrub that requires some attention to produce these magnificent blooms. Ideal for the small garden. Introduced by Guinoiseau, France, 1858.
3ft 6in × 3ft (100cm × 90cm).

'EMPEREUR DU MAROC'

'FERDINAND PICHARD'

'FERDINAND PICHARD'

One of the finest striped roses, having the advantage of a good autumn show. The medium-sized cupped flowers are pale pink with clear stripes of crimson and purple. It is most effective used as a contrast to break up the pinks and whites of a rose border. Introduced by Tanne, France, 1921.
5ft × 4ft (1.5m × 1.2m).

'GRUSS AN AACHEN'

This is a difficult rose to classify properly. It is included in this section since one of its parents was reputed to be 'Frau Karl Druski'. Flowering in clusters, 'Gruss an Aachen' has cupped flowers with many petals (84 in number), pale pink fading to cream. It has good perfume and is an excellent rose for the small garden or front of the border. Pink and white sports of this rose, as well as a climbing form, are being developed here thanks to Monsieur Daniel Schmitz of Belgium. Germany, 1909.
1ft 6in × 1ft 6in (45cm × 45cm).

'REINE DES VIOLETTES'

'SOUVENIR DU DOCTEUR JAMAIN'

'REINE DES VIOLETTES'

An unusual colour in a repeat-flowering rose, and ideal for incorporating in a mixed planting. The medium-sized flowers are a deep violet purple, fading to lilac, and opening flat with many petals. An excellent variety to grow as a climber on a grey wall. It is also a good subject for 'pegging down' (see page 122). Introduced by Millet-Mallet, France, 1860.
5ft × 3ft (1.5m × 90cm).

'SOUVENIR DU DOCTEUR JAMAIN'

This variety should be grown for the richness of its dark, almost plum-coloured flowers. It has a strong, rich perfume. Like most very dark roses it can be burnt by the sun, and is best grown in some shade. It does better in the cooler weather of autumn. It is also excellent grown as a climber, up to 3m (10ft) high, on cold, shady walls. Introduced by Lacharme, France, 1865.
5ft × 4ft (1.5m × 1.2m).

THE POLYANTHAS

Like the Chinas, these are small repeat-flowering roses, suitable for the edges of beds and any position requiring a cheerful statement. Their origin is vague, but it is thought that they arose as a cross between R. chinensis and R. multiflora. Later, many other classes were introduced into the breeding, and they subsequently gave rise to the present-day Floribundas. Their charm comes from small flowers held in clusters, which provide a tremendous display in the garden. Their habit ensures that the flowers are produced from the ground upwards.

'BLOOMFIELD ABUNDANCE'

This sport from 'Cécile Brunner' has large, delicate and feathery panicles of flowers with small, beautifully scrolled buds. It is a useful rose to grow in the middle or back of a border where this delicate effect is appreciated. More reliable than its parent in terms of habit and ease of cultivation. Introduced by Thomas, USA, 1920.
5ft × 4ft (1.5m × 1.2m).

'CÉCILE BRUNNER'

The original 'Sweetheart Rose' with exquisite pink blooms of a perfect shape. Often seen reproduced in porcelain. It is a delicate, twiggy shrub but requires some nurturing and light pruning. Introduced by Ducher, France, 1881.
2ft 6in × 2ft (75cm × 60cm).

'YVETTE'

'YVETTE'

Raised from 'Yvonne Rabier', this rose has a similar habit, with thick foliage and flowers all summer. Pale fawn-pink semi-double flowers fade to cream as they open, and have a delicate, spicy perfume. Raised by Scarman, UK, 1995.
3ft × 3ft (90cm × 90cm).

'MEVROUW NATALIE NYPELS'

One of the best varieties for late summer. The flowers are pink, with a suspicion of yellow at the base, and a charming tea-scented fragrance. A mass of stems give rise to large clusters of flowers, and the whole truss needs to be pruned as part of the deadheading regime. Introduced by Leenders, Holland, 1919.
3ft 6in × 3ft (100cm × 90cm).

'WHITE PET'

Also known as 'Little White Pet', this is a dwarf repeat-flowering sport from the rambler 'Félicité et Perpétue'. It has panicles of the same delicate, creamy-white, full

'MEVROUW NATALIE NYPELS'

petalled flowers. Excellent for pots, edging or for growing as a standard or a low hedge. Very hardy and disease-free. Introduced by Henderson, USA, 1879.
2ft 6in × 2ft (75cm × 60cm).

'YVONNE RABIER'

This rose shows the influence of *R. wichuriana* in its parentage, which contributes to the spicy fragrance. It is one of the very best white varieties, with excellent shiny, disease-free foliage and a continuity of flowering. The height depends on how vigorously it is pruned, but 3ft 6in (1m) seems to be the ideal. Introduced by Turbat, France, 1910.
3ft 6in × 2ft 6in (1m × 75cm).

'YVONNE RABIER'

THE RUGOSAS

The rugosas were brought to Europe from Japan in 1784. They are natives of coastal sand dunes and can withstand sea salt. They also seem to withstand de-icing salt on the roads, and their popularity with German municipal councils has earned them the rather derogatory term 'roundabout roses'. They are completely disease-free, require little pruning, and no deadheading because the hips are as attractive as the flowers.

The word rugosa *means 'wrinkled' in Latin, which refers to the rather coarse, veined leaves. The brown stems of rugosas are quite thorny, and it could be argued that the plants are not delicate enough to include in a small formal planting of roses but they are ideal in shrubberies, as hedges, or freestanding in grass.*

'AGNES'

'AGNES'

As a result of crossing *R. rugosa* with *R. foetida* 'Persiana', 'Agnes' is one of the few yellows available in shrub roses. The flowers are full and double with a delightful fragrance – a pleasant surprise since *foetida* means 'stinking'. The foliage is attractive but the plant does require firm pruning to keep it balanced and to avoid bare patches. It is once-flowering but may have the occasional bloom in

'ROSERIE DE L'HAY'

autumn. Introduced by Sanders, Canada, 1922. 5ft × 4ft (1.5m × 1.2m).

'BLANC DOUBLE DE COUBERT'

Claimed to have been raised from a cross with 'Sombreuil', this rose is far more likely to have been a self-pollinated white Rugosa. The ivory-white, semi-double, fragrant flowers are produced throughout the summer. The contrast between the flowers and the dark green foliage is particularly pleasing. Introduced by Cochet-Cochet, France, 1892. 6ft × 5ft (1.8m × 1.5m).

'ROSERIE DE L'HAY'

Named after the famous French rose garden, this variety has large wine-purple flowers with a rich fragrance carried on a strong shrub. The foliage is particularly pleasing in the autumn when it turns an attractive bronze-yellow. Introduced by Cochet-Cochet, France, 1901. 6ft × 6ft (1.8m × 1.8m).

'FRU DAGMAR HASTRUP'

Also known as 'Frau Dagmar Hartopp', this is one of the finest varieties to grow for its hips. Large and rounded, they are attractive at every stage from pale green through to dark red. The single pale pink flowers are fragrant and produced all summer. It makes an excellent medium-sized hedge. Germany, 1901. 4ft 6in × 4ft (1.35m × 1.2m).

'SARAH VAN FLEET'

Large, pink, semi-double flowers with a delightful scent are derived from its *R. rugosa* parentage. Flowers well

'BLANC DOUBLE DE COUBERT'

'SARAH VAN FLEET'

during the summer, and this can be improved by deadheading, since the hips will not ripen. It is a useful variety for hedging. Introduced by Dr Van Fleet, USA, 1926.
7ft × 5ft (2m × 1.5m).

THE HYBRID MUSKS

The link between Hybrid Musks and the Musk rose is tenuous, but it can be traced back through the Noisette 'Rîve d'Or', one of the great-grandparents of the cluster rose 'Trier' that eventually gave rise to this class.

The Hybrid Musks were largely developed by the Reverend Joseph Pemberton, and were first introduced in 1913 using 'Trier', a repeat-flowering climber with sprays of semi-double cream flowers, crossed with Tea roses. They are large, repeat-flowering shrubs with sprays of scented flowers held on long, arching growth. They will live to a good age, twenty years or more, but they need to be tightly pruned during the early years in order to avoid bare stems at the base. Most also make excellent climbers.

'BALLERINA'

'BALLERINA'

This rose gives the appearance of being a seedling from 'Trier', and was found by J.A. Bentall at the Reverend Pemberton's nursery. It has large trusses of single flowers, almost like a hydrangea, paler pink in the centre, and with a delicate perfume. A showy rose which is very useful for brightening up uninteresting corners. It also makes a good low Climber, for example grown under a window. Introduced by Bentall, UK, 1937.
4ft × 3ft (1.2m × 90cm).

'BUFF BEAUTY'

This is undoubtedly one of the best yellow roses. The buds, which open a deep apricot-yellow, fade to cream, giving the flowers a delightful depth of colour. The fragrant sprays are held on arching branches. Regular dead-heading will ensure a continuity of flowers. A very versatile rose, 'Buff Beauty' can be kept low, may be grown in a pot or can be encouraged to behave like a Rambler in the garden. Introduced by Pemberton, UK, 1939.
5ft × 4ft (1.5m × 1.2m).

'BUFF BEAUTY'

'CORNELIA'

'DAYBREAK'

'CORNELIA'

Large clusters of semi-double, coral-pink flowers, which fade to apricot, are held on delicate branches. One of the best varieties for autumn colour, when the flowers turn a darker shade. Excellent perfume. Introduced by Pemberton, UK, 1925.
5ft × 4ft (1.5m × 1.2m).

'DAYBREAK'

A bright and cheerful yellow rose with a dainty appearance. The flowers are semi-double and fade to cream as they age. This is a valuable variety for using in a yellow drift. Introduced by Pemberton, UK, 1918.
4ft × 3ft 6in (1.2m × 1m).

'FELICIA'

'FELICIA'

This is the most formal-shaped Hybrid Musk, and it can be used to make an attractive and productive hedge. Large, scrolled buds open pink with yellow at the base, and fade as they age to a silvery-pink. Introduced by Pemberton, UK, 1928.
5ft × 4ft (1.5m × 1.2m).

'MOONLIGHT'

'MOONLIGHT'

A repeat-flowering Hybrid
Musk, pink in the bud, with
large trusses of elegant
flowers. The white of the
flower contrasts attractively
with the dark foliage. It has a
refreshing and pleasing
perfume. Introduced by
Pemberton, UK, 1913.
5ft × 4ft (1.5m × 1.2m).

'PENELOPE'

The flowers are a mixture
of the palest pink and light
salmon, and the whole truss
has a subtle mixture of
colour. As the buds and
stamens are yellow, 'Penelope'
can be successfully used in a
yellow planting scheme.
Introduced by Pemberton,
UK, 1924.
5ft × 4ft (1.5m × 1.2m).

'THE FAIRY'

Another discovery by Bentall
at the old Pemberton nursery,
this is an excellent rose for
drifts or mass planting. The
height to which it grows
depends on the pruning, and
it is at its best kept low. Soft
pink double flowers are

'PENELOPE'

produced in large trusses and
it makes an excellent planting
companion to the lower
growing catmints. It is late
coming into flower, and
therefore excellent for
providing colour in the garden
during mid- to late summer.
Introduced by Bentall, UK,
1932.
3ft × 3ft (90cm × 90cm).

ROSE SPECIES

'MANNING'S BLUSH'

There are now about 250 roses defined as 'species' roses, but it is often difficult to determine which is or is not a species. However, there is a wide diversity among these wild roses of the northern hemisphere, and their near hybrids. Most are large plants suitable for a shrubbery or for growing freestanding in grass. The smaller varieties, like the Pimpinellifolias, can be quite invasive when established on their own roots, and because of this they are not well suited to the flower border. They also resent being pruned like other once-flowering roses. For these reasons I have not included them in the Directory of this book.

'LORD PENZANCE'

The eglantines or sweet briars (*R. eglanteria*) are natives of northern Europe. It is the scent from the foliage, reminiscent of apples, that makes these roses so worthwhile in the garden. This variety can make a huge shrub, but is at its best when grown as a column between two windows, when it will scent the whole house in early summer, especially after a shower. The small, pink, dog-rose type flowers are overlaid with yellow. Introduced by Lord Penzance, UK, 1894.
7ft × 7ft (2m × 2m) as a shrub; 12ft (3.6m) as a column.

'MANNING'S BLUSH'

This is a smaller form of the wild eglantine. The delicately pale pink flowers are double, quite small and very attractive at the bud stage. The foliage is highly scented and it is a useful plant to grow near a seat. If it is pruned too hard it will make mainly vegetative growth. UK, prior to 1799.
5ft × 4ft (1.5m × 1.2m).

R. canina

This is the native dog rose. It is a delight to grow in an informal hedge or cascading through an old fruit tree. The pale pink flowers have a fresh, clean, elusive scent, and are popular with bees. The flowers are followed by bright red hips which can be used to make a delicious rose hip syrup (See page 59).
6ft × 6ft (1.8m × 1.8m) as a shrub; 20ft (6m) or more when climbing.

'COMPLICATA'

The origins of 'Complicata' are obscure, but it is very close to a wild rose; it is possibly a cross between *R. gallica* and the dog rose *R. canina*, or otherwise a hybrid from *R. macrantha*. Vivid single flowers are borne in profusion, and a well-grown plant can look spectacular in the garden. This plant is ideal to grow at the back of a border where it can be formally pruned to put energy into the hips, which are large and rounded. Probably Middle Ages in origin.
7ft × 5ft (2m × 1.5m).

R. canina

'COMPLICATA'

R. glauca

Also known as *R. rubrifolia*. Although growing to 6ft (1.8m), the growth is delicate, and the wonderful reddish-blue foliage makes a fine contrast against pale colours. The flowers are small but the hips that follow are very dark and the earliest to form. The foliage is excellent for flower arranging. Europe, 1830.
6ft × 5ft (1.8m × 1.5m).

R. primula

It is possible that there are two forms of the 'Incense Rose' in cultivation, one of which has little discernible perfume. For years it was not listed at our nursery since our own plant carried little scent. But recently, an old plant was found and this form is highly fragrant, its leaves indeed smelling of incense. It is perfect for planting, like 'Lord Penzance', as a column between two windows, or as a large shrub in a hidden corner of the garden. The creamy-yellow, small flowers are very early. Discovered at Samarkand, Central Asia, 1910.
7ft × 6ft (2m × 1.8m) as a shrub; 12ft (3.6m) as column.

R. × richardii

Also known as *R. sancta* or 'The Holy Rose', this is one of the oldest roses in cultivation. It is believed to have been the six-petalled rose of Minoa and later Phoenicia. It was taken by the Copts in the fourth century to

R. × richardii

Abyssinia, where it was discovered at the end of the 19th century. It has a wonderful prostrate habit which creates a a low mound. The single flowers are pale pink and fade to white. A useful rose to grow down over a low wall or onto the edge of a patio. Discovered in Abyssinia, 1897.
3ft × 5ft (90cm × 1.5m).

'STANWELL PERPETUAL'

A hybrid between the 'Scotch Briar' (*R. pimpinellifolia*) and 'Autumn Damask' (*R. × damascena semperflorens*). It has small leaves which occasionally show dark markings (a characteristic of the Pimpinellifolia). The colour of the flowers depends on light levels. During the summer this is usually pale pink, fading to white; in autumn it changes, and richer pink tones evolve. Excellent fragrance. The habit is slightly untidy and it requires little or no pruning other than shaping. UK, 1838.
4ft × 4ft (1.2m × 1.2m).

'FRITZ NOBIS'

THE MODERN SHRUBS

'Modern' refers to the date of introduction rather than the parentage. In most cases this class is a result of crossing with species roses to give vigour and hardiness. Most are compatible with a planting of Old roses, and usefully extend the range of plants available, as well as providing height. They are mainly summer-flowering and once-flowering only, except for 'Golden Wings'. There is a large selection of roses in this category, though like the species from which they are derived, a number of them are too huge or too lax for a mixed planting.

'CERISE BOUQUET'

A vigorous and healthy Multibracteata hybrid that can be used as a shrub or as a rambler grown through trees; it is particularly effective in blue spruce. The semi-double cerise-crimson flowers are held in clusters on strong, wiry stems. Delicate grey-green

'CERISE BOUQUET'

foliage on powerful growth with large, triangular thorns. Introduced by Kordes, Germany, 1958.
8ft × 7ft (2.5m × 2m); 20ft (6m) climbing.

'CONSTANCE SPRY'

A large, arching shrub which needs supporting, and is at its best as a Climber. It has very large cupped flowers 4in (10cm) across, pale pink on the outside, with a deeper pink centre. It has a strong, spicy fragrance described as

myrrh. A good subject for a cold, dark wall. Introduced by Austin, UK, 1961.
6ft × 5ft (1.8m × 1.5m) as a shrub; 12ft (3.6m) climbing.

'FRITZ NOBIS'

Attractive pink flowers with some pale yellow shading at the base are quartered like an Old rose and produced with great freedom. Highly scented. 'Fritz Nobis' has an excellent habit and needs no supporting. One of the best varieties for hips. Introduced by Kordes, Germany, 1940.
5ft × 5ft (1.5m × 1.5m).

'GOLDEN WINGS'

This valuable Pimpinellifolia hybrid has large, single, primrose-yellow flowers with attractive yellow stamens which are bronze in the base. It is worth stopping any deadheading towards the end of summer to obtain the large orange hips. It may be kept low by summer pruning, but also makes an excellent Climber. It is in flower all

'CONSTANCE SPRY'

'GOLDEN WINGS'

summer. Introduced by Shepherd, USA, 1956.
4ft 6in × 3ft 6in (1.35m × 1m) as a shrub; 10ft (3m) climbing.

'MARGUERITE HILLING'
A very bushy, upright 'Nevada' sport, identical in habit and literally smothered in semi-double pink flowers in early summer. It can produce the odd flower in autumn. Raised by Hilling, UK, 1959.
7ft × 7ft (2m × 2m).

'NEVADA'
A large and dramatic shrub, covered in pale creamy-white, semi-double flowers. Both 'Marguerite Hilling' and 'Nevada' tend to 'die' badly, with petals turning brown and staying on the false hip, after a heavy shower. Despite this, they can both be extremely dramatic roses. Introduced by Dot, Spain, 1927.
7ft × 7ft (2m × 2m).

'SHROPSHIRE LASS'
An arching shrub which can equally well be grown as a Climber, with large, single cream flowers. This rose is particularly pretty in twilight and is useful to plant where it can be seen at a distance. Excellent dark red autumn hips are produced. Raised and introduced by Austin, UK, 1968.
7ft × 5ft (2m × 1.5m) grown as a shrub; 10ft (3m) grown as a climber.

'WOLLEY-DOD'
Probably a hybrid between *R. villosa* and an eglantine, this rose, also known as *R. villosa* 'Duplex', was discovered in the Reverend Wolley-Dod's garden. Its semi-double, deep rose-pink flowers held against the grey Alba-like foliage produce a beautiful, harmonious effect. Attractive dark red hips are produced in early autumn. Introduced by Wolley-Dod, UK, around 1900.
6ft × 5ft (1.8m × 1.5m).

'MARGUERITE HILLING'

'NEVADA'

'SHROPSHIRE LASS'

One of the questions I am most frequently asked is the difference between Climbers and Ramblers. Put simply, Climbers tend to have large flowers and stiffer growth, lending themselves to formal pruning, while Ramblers tend to be once-flowering, with clusters of small flowers, and long, whippy stems that are less easily controlled. The vigour of their growth varies from plant to plant.

There are, however, two groups of roses that are halfway between Climbers and Ramblers. The Noisette roses, with the exception of 'Noisette Carnée' ('Blush Noisette'), have vigorous, often untidy growth and, although classed as Climbers, behave more like Ramblers. The Barbier Ramblers ('Albéric Barbier' and 'Albertine'), on the other hand, are large-flowered, elegant plants, more suited to being grown as Climbers.

The range of Climbing roses can be dramatically extended by training shrubs as Climbers. Any free-standing Shrub rose that

will grow to 4ft (1.2m) or more can be encouraged to grow to 10ft (3m) on a wall. Even quite delicate roses like R. × odorata 'Mutabilis' or 'The Fairy' can climb well, given favourable conditions. Shrubs should be considered for use in this way when quite thick and twiggy growth is needed.

Whichever class of rose you choose, it is important that the Climber is suited to its position in the garden, and is well pruned and well presented. The choice of rose will depend on a number of factors: whether the position is sunny or shady, how protected or exposed it is, the colour and height of a wall, or the size of the garden feature which the rose is to cover. In the descriptions, I mention whether or not the plant will tolerate shade.

Pergolas and arches are delightful features in a garden, adding height and interest. Since most Climbers are repeat-flowering they make a natural choice for growing on these structures, and are usually planted in opposite pairs, with colours progressing slowly through the different shades. Experiments show that Climbers are happiest when planted with companions such as clematis, claret vines and solanums, which provide some shade and at the same time appear to make the rose less prone to disease. Pruning and tying in are critical for Climbers and Ramblers, to avoid having bare stems at the bottom and flowers only at the top.

Colour is always a matter of personal choice, but the following comments may be helpful. Just as with shrubs, pale colours show up better at a distance and particularly in early evening light. It is best to avoid too strong a contrast, for example a dark red rose like 'Guinée' against a white wall; here, the bright pink 'Madame Caroline Testout' would be more attractive, while 'Guinée' would look best against a grey stone or yellow brick wall. If space is limited, it is often more effective to plant two or three roses of the same variety, but if you do decide to mix your roses, try to combine roses of the same style, for example 'Gloire de Dijon' with 'Sombreuil', or 'Penelope' with 'Buff Beauty'. This is more important on the wall of a house than it is elsewhere. Foliage and habit are also important, particularly when the rose is not in flower. If there is other planting near the Climber, try and link the colour schemes in some way.

THE NOISETTES

These originated in America as a cross between the China rose R. × odorata 'Pallida' ('Parson's Pink China') and the Musk rose, R. × moschata. From the original seedling, 'Champneys' Pink Cluster', a Charleston nurseryman, Philippe Noisette, produced other seedlings, including 'Noisette Carnée' ('Blush Noisette'), which were sent to his brother in Paris in 1817. However, it was not until 'Champneys' Pink Cluster' was crossed with 'Parks' Yellow Tea-scented Rose' ('Parks' Yellow

China', R. × odorata 'Ochroleuca') that the typical yellowish Noisette was produced.

The first and the last two varieties listed are very vigorous, and much more like Ramblers in their habit. This comes from using 'Champneys' Pink Cluster' with R. × sempervirens; 'Champneys' Pink Cluster' is far stronger than 'Noisette Carnée', and a better seed parent. They make excellent subjects for growing through trees, but should not be chosen for walls where neatness and formality are important considerations. Their repeat-flowering ability has sometimes been overrated and they tend instead to flower in flushes.

'AIMÉE VIBERT'

Also known as 'Bouquet de la Mariée', this is best treated as a Rambler. A young plant can take three or four years before it flowers, producing an enormous amount of luxurious foliage first. This comes from its *R. sempervirens* parentage, which also contributes to its nearly evergreen habit. Perfect small white flowers are held in clusters, and it is at its finest in autumn. Introduced by Vibert, France, 1828. 20ft (6m) or more.

'CÉLINE FORESTIER'

One of the easiest Climbing roses, with a neat habit and good, regular blooming. It has acquired a reputation for tenderness that is not justified. The flowers are quartered, with pale yellow

'CÉLINE FORESTIER'

outer petals deepening to a pure yellow centre. It has an attractive Tea perfume. A useful rose to consider as a large shrub, reaching 5ft (1.5m), in a yellow drift. Introduced by Trouvillard, France, 1842. 12ft (3.6m).

'MARÉCHAL NIEL'

This rose was extensively cultivated under glass for cut flowers and Victorian posies at the turn of the century. It is ideally suited for a conservatory, and old accounts suggest planting the roots outside like a vine. The

'NOISETTE CARNÉE'

'AIMÉE VIBERT'

globular flowers are a rich yellow, with an outstanding perfume. In an unheated greenhouse it will be in flower from mid-spring right through until autumn. It is very vigorous, and unless it is treated firmly will grow huge. The best method of growing it is by pruning, in the same manner as winter pruning outdoors. The flowered shoots should be pruned immediately after flowering, to ensure a succession of healthy flushes. Introduced by Pradel, France, 1864. 10ft (3m).

'NOISETTE CARNÉE'

This charming plant, also known as 'Blush Noisette', is equally at home grown as a shrub to 5ft (1.5m). It has sprays of delightful semi-double pink flowers which are produced regularly throughout the summer. The very attractive, spicy fragrance comes from the Musk rose. This is one of the best roses to grow where a soft Rambler effect is required– on an arbour for example. Introduced by Noisette, France, 1817. 10ft (3m).

'DESPREZ À FLEURS JAUNES'

'DESPREZ À FLEURS JAUNÈS'

This is also known as 'Jaune Desprez'. The first flush of flowers are yellow, shaded with pink; they are quite small, and held in groups of three or four, with a strong Tea perfume. As the summer progresses the flowers tend to lose their pink shading. The growth is quite rampant and it is ideally suited to being grown through a fruit tree. Introduced by Desprez, France, 1826.
20ft (6m).

'MADAME ALFRED CARRIÈRE'

This rose combines Noisette vigour with large, white, Tea-shaped flowers which, opening pale pink, quickly turn white. They have a refreshing, strong perfume. It can cover a large area and produces a great many stems. When grown on a wall the vegetative shoots need to be pruned at least three times in summer to maintain a neat appearance. Introduced by Schwartz, France, 1879.
20ft (6m).

'MADAME ALFRED CARRIÈRE'

THE TEAS

The original Tea roses, so named because their perfume from R. odorata has a fragrance of freshly harvested tea, came into Europe at the beginning of the nineteenth century. 'Parks' Yellow Tea-scented Rose' (R.× odorata 'Ochroleuca') was responsible for introducing yellow into this group. Hybridization with other classes gave rise to the bitter-sweet perfume which is particularly notable in 'Gloire de Dijon'. The early Tea roses have long pointed and scrolled buds, and a delicate growth that belies their vigour. Most are better suited to warmer climates, though the varieties listed below are all hardy in temperate zones.

'LADY HILLINGDON'

The long, elegant, scrolled buds of a warm, rich apricot-yellow open to yellow flowers. The foliage is bronze-tinted and stems are reddish, offering an attractive contrast. One of the best examples of the Tea perfume. In flower all summer. Introduced by Hicks, UK, 1917.
15ft (4.5m).

'MRS HERBERT STEVENS'

The long, elegant buds are typical of the original Teas. The flowers are pure white with a hint of green, and have a good Tea fragrance. It flowers once in the summer, with an occasional bloom in the autumn. Introduced by Pernet-Ducher, France, 1922.
15ft (4.5m).

'LADY HILLINGDON'

'SOMBREUIL'

This rose has Bourbon parentage, and its habit and form place it nearer to that group. It is a mystery why this beautiful rose is not better known and more widely grown. The richly perfumed white flowers are large, with lots of petals in a quartered arrangement, and open with a hint of pink before forming a flat shape. It flowers all summer. Dark green foliage is etched with bronze. Hardy and easy to grow. Introduced by Robert, France, 1851.
12ft (3.6m).

'SOMBREUIL'

'SOUVENIR DE MADAME LÉONIE VIENNOT'

'SOUVENIR DE MADAME LÉONIE VIENNOT'

A vigorous rose, but its straggly growth makes it difficult to grow well. It is worth it for the most exceptional flowers, which are pale apricot with fine veins of deep pink that seem to owe more to the artist's fine brush than to nature. It produces occasional autumn blooms. The best situation for this rose is a shaded wall or other garden structure. Introduced by Bernaix, France, 1897.
15ft (4.5m).

THE BOURBONS

The climbing bourbons resulted from crosses between Bourbons, Teas and Noisettes. They are good subjects for formal pruning and most of them flower throughout the summer. It is important to keep them fanned out, with the outer branches as low as possible.

'BLAIRII NUMBER TWO'
'Blairii Number One' was less refined, but this once-flowering rose shows to perfection one of the most enduring traits of the older varieties: the outer petals are

of the palest pink and deepen towards the centre to a warm, rich pink. It is a good variety for a shady wall or arch. Some authorities suggest that it resents hard pruning, but in my experience this appears to be unfounded. Introduced by Blair, UK, 1845.
12ft (3.6m).

'GLOIRE DE DIJON'
There are few roses that are still just as exciting 140 years or more after their date of introduction but this rose, also known as 'Old Glory', is one. In bloom all summer long, the large, globe-shaped flowers hang downwards so they can be appreciated from the ground. Their colour is predominantly yellow, but

'GLOIRE DE DIJON' ('OLD GLORY')

suffused with warm tones of salmon and pink. Its seed parent was probably 'Souvenir de la Malmaison', but the rich fragrance is overlaid with a slightly bitter note that reveals its Tea origins. Introduced by Jacotot, France, 1853.
12ft (3.6m).

'BLAIRII NUMBER TWO'

'ZÉPHIRINE DROUHIN'

'GUINÉE'

'MADAME CAROLINE TESTOUT'

'ZÉPHIRINE DROUHIN'

Well known as the 'thornless' rose, it may nevertheless have a few thorns hidden away as a surprise. The flowers are a bright, deep rose-pink with a warm and haunting fragrance. It thrives on a shady wall, where it may resist mildew. It is also a good choice as a shrub to 5ft (1.5m). Introduced by Bizot, France, 1868.
12ft (3.6m).

THE HYBRID TEAS

Most of the early Hybrid Teas produced Climbing sports that were often more reliable than the shrub. They are easy to train and prune in a formal manner, and provide repeat-flowering pinks and dark reds not available in the other Climbing classes, unless shrubs are considered.

'GUINÉE'

This is one of the best of the very dark red Climbers. The flowers are deep velvet crimson with outstanding perfume. 'Guinée' will set

hips, so the amount of deadheading that is carried out will dictate how much it will repeat. A useful variety against grey or dull-coloured walls. Introduced by Mallerin, France, 1938.
12ft (3.6m)

'MADAME CAROLINE TESTOUT'

The flowers are a deep rich pink with a globular shape.

Like all this class, good fan training will result in a productive Climber; it will otherwise shoot up with immense vigour. Introduced by Chauvry, France, 1901.
12ft (3.6m).

'MADAME GRÉGOIRE STAECHELIN'

Although flowering only once, its vigour and huge

quantity of flowers make this a must on any pale-coloured wall. The flowers are a rich pink with paler edges, and hang downwards. It produces large orange hips in the autumn. Raised by Dot, Spain, 1927. Introduced in America as 'Spanish Beauty'.
20ft (6m).

'MADAME GRÉGOIRE STAECHELIN'

'POMPON DE PARIS'

THE CHINA

This is a Climbing sport from one of the original China roses, R. chinensis minima, *the ancestor of the Miniature roses.*

'POMPON DE PARIS'
Despite having tiny leaves and flowers, similar in colour to *R. × odorata* 'Pallida' ('Old Blush', 'Parson's Pink China'), this rose is multi-stemmed and very vigorous. It should be considered where a dense covering is needed. Once established it will repeat-flower. Origin date unknown. 15ft (4.5m).

THE BRACTEATA

Crossed with a yellow Tea rose, 'Mermaid' carries the same glossy foliage and strong thorny habit as R. bracteata.

'MERMAID'
The flowers are large, single, with warm, rich, sulphur-yellow petals and contrasting mahogany stamens. It will flower all summer, but requires a warm and sheltered wall, and should be grown only by those brave enough to deal with the powerful thorny growth. Introduced by Paul, UK, 1918. 20ft (6m).

'MERMAID'

RAMBLING ROSES

'BOBBIE JAMES'

Rambling roses are very versatile. They can be used either for formal training on structures or, more informally, for tumbling, wild planting. The same variety can often be used for either effect, the only difference being in the pruning. 'Albéric Barbier', for example, can luxuriate along a fence or be tightly pruned and trained on pillar and ropes. You can also use Ramblers to hang down and weep, when they will produce a cascading waterfall of colour. Old fruit trees, dividing walls or unsightly buildings all make good frames. Although almost all Ramblers flower only once during the summer, their sheer quantity of flowers cannot be equalled, and colour can always be extended by growing late-flowering clematis with them. Most Ramblers have thick growth and fine foliage, which give a solid appearance all year round.

THE SPECIES

The different classes into which Ramblers are divided mostly follow the species from which they evolved. These classes are useful in helping us to understand the different habit of the roses, and this in turn will indicate appropriate planting positions.

'BOBBIE JAMES'
Although usually listed as a Multiflora, the habit of this rose is far closer to that of *R. filipes*. It is a charming rose, with large, semi-double creamy-white flowers with a strong and refreshing perfume. It is happy covering a large barn or growing through a substantial tree, although the rose in my garden (shown in the photograph, left) is contained on an 8ft (2.5m) arch by tight pruning. Introduced by Sunningdale Nurseries, UK, 1961.
30ft (9m).

'BRENDA COLVIN'
This is probably a seedling from 'Kiftsgate'. It is a powerful rose which can nevertheless be tamed on a large wall. The flowers are a soft pink with yellow stamens, giving a pale apricot effect. The blooms are held in large clusters and their fragrance is successfully carried on the wind. It was found outside Brenda Colvin's offices. Introduced by Colvin, UK, 1970.
30ft (9m).

'BRENDA COLVIN'

R. banksiae 'LUTEA'
This is the first rose to come into flower, with billowing masses of double yellow flowers held in hanging sprays. It is a vigorous plant, easy to train, and needs only light pruning after flowering in mid- to late summer. The foliage is very handsome when the rose is not in flower. Not hardy below -12°C.
Introduced from China, 1825.
20ft × 20ft (6m × 6m).

R. filipes 'KIFTSGATE'
The largest and most powerful of all the Ramblers was found as a seedling at Kiftsgate Court in England. It can attain huge dimensions, and is ideal to grow through a large tree or to create a dramatic statement. Enormous panicles of small, scented, creamy-white flowers are followed by thousands of small hips. Introduced by Murrell, UK, 1954.
50ft (15m) or more.

R. filipes 'KIFTSGATE'

'THE BISHOP'S RAMBLER'

This was raised from 'Wedding Day' but is less pendulous in habit. The flowers are an unusual colour for a Rambler, opening dark red with contrasting bright yellow stamens, and fading to purple as they age. It is an interesting rose to use on an obelisk or pillar, surrounded by a purple drift of companion planting. It has an attractive fragrance and disease-free foliage. Introduced by Scarman, UK, 1995.
15ft (4.5m).

'WEDDING DAY'

There is some doubt as to the origin of this rose; it may be a *R. longicuspis* or *R. sinowilsonii* hybrid. It has a wonderful trailing habit and is ideal to grow over a wall or building where it can be allowed to tumble down on the other side. The buds are creamy-yellow, fading to white, and the flowers are held in large trusses. It has attractive shiny foliage and a terrific autumn display of tiny red hips. The perfume is exceptional and carries well on the wind. Introduced by Stern, UK, 1950.
30ft (9m) or more.

THE MULTIFLORAS

These are hybrids developed at the end of the nineteenth century from a native Japanese rose. The young stems are strong and upright, and plants in this group are well suited for growing on walls and arches. The foliage is pale green and the flowers are held in large panicles. They provide very useful colours — dusky purples and pale lilacs — which, when combined with dark red or striped roses, produce interesting contrasts.

'BLEU MAGENTA'

The flowers open a rich red-purple and rapidly fade to a dusky purple. The Belgian honeysuckle makes an excellent planting companion, with the same colour in the bud before the flowers open to yellow. So, too, do Shrub roses like 'Tuscany Superb' and 'Reine des Violettes'. Introduced in Germany, 1899.
15ft (4.5m).

'GOLDFINCH'

This is one of the few yellows among the small-flowered Ramblers. The buds are bright yellow and fade to cream,

'VEILCHENBLAU'

'GOLDFINCH'

with a strong, rich fragrance. It is not too vigorous and makes a charming subject for an arch. The flowers are followed in the autumn by a fine crop of small red hips. Introduced by Paul, UK, 1907.
12ft (3.6m).

'VEILCHENBLAU'

An intriguing rose, with individual flowers changing from magenta to lilac and grey as they age. The effect depends on light levels, but from a distance it can appear in strong sunlight to be a pale grey-blue. The flowers have a delicate fruity fragrance. It is most effective used as a contrast with striped roses like 'Variegata di Bologna', or with yellows. Introduced by Schmidt, Germany, 1909.
15ft (4.5m).

'PAUL'S HIMALAYAN MUSK'

THE MUSKS

The original Musk rose, R. moschata, is an elusive and mysterious rose with a hidden past. It was first described in Persia in the tenth century, where it was cultivated for its perfume which is pungent, gingery and persuasive, and used to make rose water. The Musk rose played an important part in the cut-flower industry in the fifteenth century and is known to have been introduced into England from Spain and to have been growing in England by around 1521. It is recorded in Germany and France later in the sixteenth century, and was probably introduced from the Middle East. Then it disappeared.

Yet it was at that time the only late-summer flowering rose; it was a good rose; and it was scented. (Musks are the only roses that are scented in the late afternoon; if flowers are picked in tight bud in the morning and placed indoors, by the evening they have opened and filled a room with perfume.) So why, or how, did it disappear?

In A Midsummer Night's Dream, written at the end of the sixteenth century, Titania sleeps on a bank among scented flowers,
"Quite over-canopied ...
With sweet musks roses and with eglantine."

Learned scholars propose, among other suggestions, that Shakespeare may be referring to the field rose, Rosa arvensis, but the field rose has no scent. Ever in favour of simple solutions, I cannot help wondering if Shakespeare did not know exactly what he was talking about.

Musk roses appear in many different varieties and sports, but they exist in two forms only: an early summer Rambler and a late-summer flowering Shrub. Today, the plant offered as R. moschata differs from grower to grower.

I became convinced that the original R. moschata either reverted or sported into something else and that the most likely candidate for the original plant is what is now known as 'Rambling Rector'. This rose is listed as a Multiflora, yet even a cursory examination of the foliage, thorns and perfume makes this an unlikely attribution; it bears a far closer resemblance to roses described as Musks.

To test my theory, a close eye was kept on this rose to see if it sported (not all roses do), and in September 1990 a sport was found at Ingestre in Staffordshire, England. This seemed to prove my theory that R. moschata had reverted – and had reverted to 'Rambling Rector'. It is this sport that I now grow here as R. moschata. And 'Rambling Rector' may, if my claim is correct, be Shakespeare's Musk rose.

Whatever it may have been, R. moschata played a significant part in the early breeding of roses; and more recently with the Noisettes and Hybrid Musks. The value of the Musks lies both in their scent and in the fact that they start to flower in the middle of summer and last well into autumn. Long after other Rambling roses have finished flowering, the Musks continue. They make untidy shrubs, and are best grown on a support on a wall, but are valuable at this time, when the once-flowering roses are over and most repeat-flowering roses are resting.

'KIRSTEN KLEIN'

'KIRSTEN KLEIN'

A Moschata hybrid which has the power of 'Rambling Rector' combined with the late flowering of R. moschata. Its habit is that of a Rambler, but it could easily be grown on a wall. The rose-pink flowers are quite large and held in conspicuous trusses. The perfume is outstanding and, like most single roses, carried well on the breeze. Both 'Kirsten Klein' and 'The Lady Scarman' are worth considering for their late flowering. 'Kirsten Klein' is disease-free, with thorny stems and typical Rambler foliage. Raised by Baden Fergusson and introduced by Scarman, UK, 1995. 12ft (3.6m).

'PAUL'S HIMALAYAN MUSK'
Reputed to have been a hybrid from *R. brunonii*, this is a most attractive rose. The flowers are rose-pink on opening, with lots of petals, and as they age they fade to white. The entire plant is covered in differing shades of pink and white. It has a strong Musk fragrance, and an easy habit which, despite strong growth, make it an excellent choice for large structures. Introduced by Paul, UK, 1918. 30ft (9m).

R. brunonii
Originally, and probably correctly, described as *R. moschata* var. *nepalensis*, this rose has an attractive and delicate balance between flowers, foliage and, later on, the hips. It appears to be a single-flowered form of 'Rambling Rector', with enlarged flowers as a result. It is far hardier than early accounts suggest. Nepal, 1820. 30ft (9m).

'THE LADY SCARMAN'
This is a hybrid between *R. moschata* and 'Noisette Carnée' (itself a seedling of *R. moschata* and *R. chinensis*). The idea was to produce

'THE LADY SCARMAN'

R. moschata in a more amenable and biddable form. The semi-double flowers are pale cream, with the intense, pervading Musk perfume. The foliage is disease-free, and the growth easy to train on a wall, arch or pillar. It starts to flower in late summer, and continues until the autumn. Introduced by Scarman, UK, 1995. 10ft (3m).

'RAMBLING RECTOR'
Whether 'Rambling Rector' or *R. moschata* was the original plant is a little like the chicken and egg, though probability puts 'Rambling Rector' first (see the introduction to The Musks, page 98). Although very vigorous, it is quite easy to contain on a wall or structure. The semi-double white flowers are quite small, and the yellow stamens give it a creamy appearance. The Musk fragrance is intense, and the flowers are followed by small, oval-shaped orange hips. A very old variety. 30ft (9m) or more.

'RAMBLING RECTOR'

R. brunonii

The Sempervirens

These hybrids were raised from the 'evergreen' rose, a native European species. The Ramblers in this class differ from others in having an enormous number of branches with thin stems. The foliage is disease-free and is, in all but the hardest winters, evergreen, and the thick mat that it forms makes a striking contrast to the pale flowers. These Ramblers are quite delicate in habit, with naturally pendulous stems. This allows them to be used in any position where a trailing habit is desirable: tumbling over walls, down banks, or in any position where you want to create a wild look.

'Adélaïde d'Orléans'
Despite a delicate appearance, this is a vigorous and dependable rose. It has many uses and is very good for softening the sharp outline of trellis. The flowers open creamy-pink and fade to white. The perfume is light and reminiscent of primroses. Introduced by Jacques, France, 1826.
15ft (4.5m).

'Félicité et Perpétue'
The densest of all Ramblers, and ideal to use as a cascade. Planted on the shady side of a wall, it will rapidly grow up and then tumble over the other side. The flowers are small, well filled with petals, and creamy-white, opening rapidly from pink buds. It was a great favourite of Gertrude

'Adélaïde d'Orléans'

'Félicité et Perpétue'

Jekyll, and was named after the Carthaginian martyrs. Introduced by Jacques, France, 1827.
20ft (6m).

The Wichurianas

The Barbier hybrids retain the shiny foliage and long, arching branches of the original Chinese species. Their large, well filled flowers come from crossing with Tea roses. They differ considerably in habit, depending on the hybridization, but they offer a different style from other Ramblers, and their habit and large flowers place them nearer the Climbing roses.

'Albertine'
This well known Rambler is to be found in nearly every cottage garden. The buds are coppery-pink and open to large flowers of a rich pink with a strong perfume. It is a good subject for difficult and cold positions. The habit is quite flexible and it can be grown along low ropes as well as on a wall. Introduced by Barbier, France, 1921.
20ft (6m).

'Albéric Barbier'
This is a valuable variety because of its pendulous growth which makes it easy to train lengthways along a low wall or fence. It is one of the best for using on swags and pillars. The flowers are yellow in the bud and fade to cream as they open, with a soft perfume. It has excellent

'ALBERTINE'

'ALBÉRIC BARBIER'

'MAY QUEEN'

shiny, disease-free foliage. Introduced by Barbier, France, 1900.
20ft (6m).

'LÉONTINE GERVAIS'
A good companion to 'Albéric Barbier'; habit, foliage and growth all complement each other well. The flowers are predominantly pink, well filled with petals that have light shades of yellow at the base. The fragrance is particularly rich, with Tea rose overtones. When established, it seems to flower continuously, especially if deadheaded. Introduced by Barbier, France, 1903.
20ft (6m).

'MAY QUEEN'
A free-flowering Rambler with masses of medium-sized rich pink flowers with a swirling arrangement of petals. The dainty appearance of this rose belies its vigour and hardiness, and its twiggy nature and pendulous habit offer a number of different planting uses, especially on pergolas and arbours. Introduced by Manda, USA, 1898.
15ft (4.5m).

'BREWOOD BELLE'

'MRS BILLY CRICK'

'NEW DAWN'

REPEAT-FLOWERING RAMBLERS

These are some of the most useful and valuable roses, especially in the smaller garden where space is at a premium and everything has to work over the longest possible period.

Ramblers are by nature once-flowering, and the process of raising a repeat-flowering Rambler is not simple. You must first cross one Rambler with a repeat-flowering rose, and another Rambler with another

repeat-flowering rose. When these crosses flower, some three or four years later, they must be crossed with each other. Even if all that works, the results can be quite variable.

The ability to repeat-flower diminishes the Rambling vigour, and this group will rarely exceed 8ft (2.5m) in height. As a result, they are ideally suited for formal pruning on walls and structures.

'BREWOOD BELLE'
The flowers are quite small, well filled with petals, and held in clusters. The colour is

a bright coral-pink which does not fade with age. Regular deadheading is important, since this variety will set hips. A useful rose for a pillar or obelisk against a dull background. Introduced by Scarman, UK, 1995.
10ft (3m).

'MRS BILLY CRICK'
The dainty single flowers open a warm pink, with white centres and yellow stamens. The older flowers fade to a pale pink, and the cluster is

always in several shades of pink. They have a delicate perfume. This rose looks perfect in a cottage garden. Introduced by Scarman, UK, 1995.
8ft (2.5m).

'NEW DAWN'
A repeat-flowering Wichuriana Rambler of considerable vigour. It is a sport from 'Dr van Fleet' and has the same pale pink flowers, with an attractive shape and fruity perfume. The amount that it repeats is dictated by

'PHYLLIS BIDE'

deadheading, and the pruning of its powerful vegetative shoots. Introduced by the Somerset Rose Company, USA, 1930.
20ft (6m).

'PHYLLIS BIDE'
The buds of this Multiflora China hybrid open a light orange, and the pale yellow semi-double flowers are overlaid with pink. It is useful for growing over arches, where its delicate twiggy growth makes a dense cover.

Most arches will need four plants: two roses planted on each side. Introduced by Bide, UK, 1923.
8ft (2.5m).

'WHITE WEDDING'
The flowers are creamy-yellow in the bud, and open to white single flowers held in small clusters, reminiscent of 'Wedding Day'. It forms pretty hips in the autumn, and needs regular deadheading until the end of summer. Introduced by Scarman, UK, 1995.
8ft (2.5m).

'WHITE WEDDING'

caring
for Old
Roses

PRUNING OLD ROSES

Old roses are very versatile: they can be tightly pruned in the formal garden or left unpruned, billowing in the orchard. The timing of pruning will also depend on the type and class of the rose.

PRUNING ONCE-FLOWERING SHRUB ROSES

Summer-flowering Old Shrub roses flower over a period of five to six weeks in the summer months. The performance, shape, texture and reliability of once-flowering varieties is much more rewarding than that of repeat-flowering Shrubs. They have many more branches, with thicker foliage, and when well pruned will flower from the ground up.

The principles of pruning are the same for virtually all summer-flowering Old Shrub roses, regardless of whether they are Gallicas, Albas, Centifolias, Damasks or Moss roses. Only the Species and the Modern Shrub roses are treated differently (see below). There is no need to be over-cautious or lacking in confidence when pruning Old roses. It is very straightforward, and with practice quite fast; you cannot go very far wrong, provided you keep reasonably closely to the timing indicated.

Old once-flowering roses should not be pruned like Hybrid Teas. With Old roses it would be nearly impossible, because of the sheer number of branches, to prune to an outward-facing bud, nor do they need the old wood in the centre pruning out, unless it has ceased to be productive. The original wild Species roses, which evolved thousands of years ago and which the Old roses closely resemble, had their own defence against being browsed by herbivores: the shoot simple died back to the nearest bud, creating a snag or short stump.

We prune our once-flowering Old roses three times a year, with the object

of improving both the shape and the productivity of the plants. As far as the shrub's overall shape is concerned, the aim is to produce a curved dome of growth, rather than a cone-shaped shrub, and this in turn will help the plant to flower from the base up.

(top) Once-flowering 'Ispahan' before pruning, in early summer. Flowers are being produced but the overall growth of the shrub is untidy.

(above) The first pruning directs the rose's energy into the production of flowers. It improves the shape of the shrub and allows the flowers to be seen.

FIRST PRUNING

The first pruning of the year is in early summer, although the exact time will depend on the weather and the geographic position and climate. A safe indicator is when the calyx splits, which is when the flower bud opens sufficiently to show some colour.

At this stage the Shrub will have two types of growth. The first is covered in flower buds and the second is vegetative growth. If the vegetative growth is allowed to remain, it will hide the flowers and detract from the architectural appearance of the plant, as well as taking up most of the plant's energy. When it is cut back to the level of the flowers (the flowering height), which is a quick and simple job (forget about cutting directly above or below a bud), the energy of the plant is directed solely to the flowers, and its appearance is greatly improved.

We regularly deadhead these roses, pinching out single spent blooms, to put the energy into the next flowering buds. However, with varieties that set hips, such as *R. gallica* 'Versicolor' ('Rosa Mundi'), we simply brush off the dead petals, leaving the hips intact.

SECOND PRUNING

The second pruning is done in very late summer, and this time it is done for architectural appearance. The dead flowers or hips (depending on the variety) will now be hidden by a dense growth of young vegetative shoots, and these are often a target of mildew to which the older leaves will be immune (a natural phenomenon which can be observed in many plant species: the oak, for example). This growth is again pruned back to the height of the flowers, leaving a neat shrub which, if it is a hipping variety, will then develop hips in a stronger manner than usual. Any growth that has been bowed down by the weight of the flowers (Gallicas are particularly susceptible to this) should also be vigorously pruned; the growth will soon spring back up, and next year's flowers will come from the next bud down on each stem.

(top) 'Pompon de Bourgogne' frames a seating area. Before its late summer pruning it has produced a mass of young vegetative shoots.

(above) Late summer pruning will secure the rose during the winter. It will also increase the basal shoots and improve the garden's appearance.

The summer pruning of vegetative shoots has the effect of significantly increasing the number of stems in the body of the shrub, and therefore the number of flowers the following year. Since most of these stems are produced low down from mature wood, it is unnecessary (indeed, it is a mistake) to remove old wood unless it is no longer productive.

Another advantage of pruning at this time is that the rose will be secured against autumn gales and subsequent wind rock (all the more so if it was not planted well below the union of scion and stock in the first place). It will also be less prone to snow damage, and there will be fewer mature leaves left to provide overwintering places for disease spores — although Old roses tend in any case to lose their leaves comparatively early in the season.

FINAL PRUNING

The final pruning is done at any time between autumn and spring; unlike Hybrid Teas, it makes no difference when this is done. By pruning earlier, you will reduce the workload in early spring, and if the roses are underplanted with bulbs it is anyway advisable to do it well before they come up.

This pruning is carried out to what is known as the pruning height. The photographs show the summer flowering height and the pruning height. The rose illustrated, 'Félicité Parmentier', can easily become untidy unless it is firmly pruned. Any snags should also be removed to ensure that there are no overwintering places for sawfly (a snag with a hole in the centre denotes their presence), and twiggy dead growth near the bottom or centre of the shrub should be removed. It is not necessary to thin out the central growth if it is still being productive.

Growth that has become bowed over, especially after a summer storm, should be pruned back when it happens. Provided it is done by late summer, the shrub will quickly spring back into shape.

It is time for winter pruning of the Alba, 'Félicité Parmentier'. Pruning back to the previous season's pruning height will create a dense, twiggy framework which is self-supporting.

The pruning should be carried out to a dome-shape, rather than flat on top. Growth lower down at the front should be encouraged in order to avoid bare stems. With Old once-flowering roses the flowering is not diminshed by this, provided the appropriate summer pruning has also taken place.

When establishing young roses there is a temptation to let them get to their full height in one season. It is important to resist this temptation! When the rose is winter-pruned it should be allowed to gain no more than 6in (15cm) in height. This will allow the development of strong branches, and a dense framework for further years. The rose should be pruned in this way (approximately halfway between the flowering height and the regular pruning height) until it has reached its final height. The approximate eventual height of the roses is given in the Directory entries later in the book, though exactly how high a rose is allowed to grow will depend to a large extent on its position in the garden, and on how floppy the growth of a particular species or variety is.

There are inevitably a few exceptions to these general principles. The large Species roses and their near hybrids, the Modern Shrub roses, are as a rule sufficiently robust to stand on their own, whether in grass or in a border of mixed shrubs, without need of supports (see page 113) or pruning. But they will tend to send out long shoots that carry the following year's flowers, and if they do need pruning, because of their planting position in the garden, they should be treated exactly as other Old roses. Some of their more vigorous near hybrids, however, may need either supports or pruning.

It is also possible with some varieties of Old shrub roses ('Ispahan' or 'Madame Hardy', for example) to let the long stems develop and then tie them down to imitate the shape of the bush. This can be unsightly while the stem is developing, and it does detract from the production of flowers lower down. It is in fact better to extend this idea, and adopt the art of pegging down the entire plant (see page 122).

When Shrub roses become overgrown, a firm hand is needed to establish a new pruning height. However, you should retain the twiggy framework and not thin out any of the branches, except for dead wood.

Winter pruning enables you to assess the outline of the Shrub and to take its overall shape into account. This shrub has been reduced to a manageable size but will flower the next season.

Stopping young shoots near the base will encourage flowers to be produced from ground level upwards in order to avoid bare stems. This only applies to the outside of the shrub: young shoots in the middle should be pruned to the overall pruning height.

PRUNING SUMMARY

Summer:
Prune vegetative shoots as soon as the calyx of flowers splits to show some colour.

Late summer to early autumn:
Prune all vegetative shoots and any bowed branches back to flowering height to within two buds, always keeping the required overall shape of the plant in mind.

Winter to early spring:
Remove any snags and dead wood; prune down to the pruning height and aim for a good architectural shape.

REPEAT-FLOWERING SHRUB ROSES

There are many excellent books on Hybrid Teas and Floribundas, but the pruning methods required for the repeat-flowering Old Shrub roses are rather different, although the principle that every shoot will develop into a flower remains generally true. As with all repeat-flowering roses, deadheading is important, though this is often done in combination with summer pruning. Only Rugosas should not be summer pruned, as their hips are of just as much value in the garden as their flowers. Towards the end of the summer, you should also stop deadheading other varieties (such as 'Golden Wings') that set attractive hips.

The key to the pruning of repeat-flowering roses is continuous light summer pruning and deadheading, autumn pruning to shape the plant and prevent wind rock and snow damage, and detailed pruning for shape in winter or early spring. As with the once-flowering varieties, winter pruning should take the shrubs back to the pruning height. Dead wood should also be removed.

It is important, as with all roses, to start pruning a young plant from its first year. By the end of the first year, repeat-flowering roses should have several stems, and in winter these should be pruned back and shaped to a dome no more than 6in (15cm) higher than when you received the plant. Any particularly twiggy rose should have its stems halved in height. Summer pruning and vigorous deadheading will encourage the young plant to thicken up and to shoot from the base. As they develop, these basal shoots may need to be stopped and broken (this means simply pinching out the growing tip of the young shoot). This needs to be done either to promote branching, or

(top) To fill the corner of a bed, five repeat-flowering Shrub roses ('De Rescht') have been planted in a drift and they will need to be pruned with their shape and overall effect firmly in mind.

(above) The object of pruning this repeat-flowering Shrub rose is to keep the front and sides as low as possible and to taper them towards the centre. This will provide flowers as low down as possible to help round off the sharp architectural edge of the corner.

encourage the production of a greater number of flowers, and to maintain the overall shape of the shrub.

PORTLAND DAMASKS

These roses have the foliage and habit of Old roses, plus the ability to flower in flushes, normally three times in the summer. The trick is constant deadheading and summer pruning of flowered shoots to two buds beneath the spent flower. This summer pruning should be quite light, because subsequent flowers will be produced more quickly higher up the flowering stem than they would be lower down. Winter pruning should at least halve the growth made during the summer, shortening it to just above the previous winter's pruning height.

BOURBONS AND HYBRID PERPETUALS

The majority of the roses in this group are quite vigorous and upright in their habit, and the pruning instructions given below apply to them. The smaller-growing roses, however, should be pruned in exactly the same way as the Chinas and Polyanthas, so it is important to check the size of the particular rose in the Directory (see pages 77–80).

The larger Shrubs quite often send out long shoots which destroy the overall shape of the plant, and for this reason they make excellent Climbers and Pillar roses. To keep the plant as a shrub, these shoots should be stopped and broken as they appear, which will result in later flowers from this wood. Deadheading and subsequent light summer pruning are vital to ensure a succession of flowers, and the more this is done, the more they will repeat-flower. If it is carried out only occasionally, the plant will tend to flower in flushes.

In autumn the plants should be shaped, and any long stems reduced. Pruning

This shows a Bourbon rose, 'Madame Pierre Oger', before pruning. Unlike a modern Hybrid Tea, the growth should not be thinned out. Summer deadheading should be carried out to within two or three buds from the pruning height.

The same repeat-flowering Shrub rose, after pruning. By retaining all the stems, there will be more flowers produced, but their size will be slightly smaller.

A close-up of the pruning height shows how close it is carried out to the previous season's pruning height. It also makes the point that neatness and attention to detail are more important than the direction in which the buds face. Prune the centre of the rose at an even height.

proper is carried out in spring, early or late depending on the weather and local geography. The object of hard winter pruning is to encourage the plants to produce as many stems as possible. Keeping them pruned low and tight will prevent any bare stems at the base of the shrub and avoid producing a tall, thin plant with slender stems that may be unable to bear the weight of its flowers.

CHINAS AND POLYANTHAS

Chinas and Polyanthas both tend to be small, rather twiggy plants, which resent firm pruning. Pruning is therefore best done by means of deadheading as a form of summer pruning. When all the flowers on a stem have finished flowering, the entire stem is pruned down to half its length. Although it is worth taking the trouble to prune just above a bud (the direction in which it is facing is unimportant), the pruning should always be done with an eye to the architectural appearance of the shrub. Twiggy growth can and should be retained since it will produce one or two flowers which will enhance the display.

Polyanthas differ from Chinas in having large trusses of Rambler-like flowers. When the flowers are over, the entire truss should be removed down to the first bud on the stem; this will then produce further trusses.

Winter pruning for both classes of rose involves a final deadheading and the removal of dead wood. The shrubs should then be cut back to the previous season's flowering height and generally shaped for neatness.

RUGOSAS

Rugosa means 'wrinkled' in Latin, and refers to the leathery, veined leaves. Originally natives of Japanese sand dunes, these sturdy shrubs will withstand sea spray and de-icing salt equally well. Since they are grown both for their flowers and their hips, they should not be pruned during the summer. Pruning either in winter or spring needs to be quite fierce, almost down to the previous year's height. This will encourage young basal growth, and will prevent bare stems at the bottom. Some of these strong basal shoots may be left to reach the height of the shrub, and others, especially those occurring on the outside of

The Polyantha 'Yvonne Rabier' is a variety which can become large and untidy unless it is kept in check by regular pruning.

By retaining the twiggy growth, the rose's energy is evenly distributed and the growth is therefore more manageable.

the shrub, should be cut back in winter to produce flowers lower down.

HYBRID MUSKS

This fascinating group of roses show their Rambler parentage in the long, arching branches covered in clusters of fragrant flowers. There are two types of flowering growth: huge trusses held away from the shrub, and small, twiggy flowering stems with a few blooms. Both types should be deadheaded in summer to maintain the flowering succession. Summer pruning of the huge trusses is especially important; these

should be pruned right back straight after flowering, to within one or two buds of the main stem. The shrubs should be lightly pruned and shaped in the autumn, and more formal pruning can then be carried out the following spring.

This group of roses is prone to bare, woody stems, particularly if they are not pruned during their first years. However, once they are established they need very little pruning: just summer pruning in the form of deadheading, with the occasional basal shoot cut in order to maintain the production of flowers lower down.

MODERN SHRUB ROSES

The Modern English roses combine the flower shape of Old roses with the habit and foliage of Floribundas. The weight of the flowers can be too great for the stems, particularly in wet weather. They need vigorous summer pruning to reduce stem length, as for the Bourbons.

Summer pruning a truss on a Modern Shrub rose.

GROUND-COVER ROSES

Having seen what happens when creeping thistles and couch grass get a hold underneath Ground-cover roses, I have a slight prejudice against this class. They are at their best on banks, or growing down over low walls or steps. They respond well to being tidied up in early spring, by removing dead wood and accumulated wind-blown leaves from underneath them.

CLIMBING ROSES

The pruning of Climbing roses is closely linked to the way they are trained, and if properly trained, roses grown against walls are one of the most rewarding sights in the garden. The aim should be to achieve a fan shape against the wall, with the branches of the rose tied in in sequence, to avoid crossing branches, and the plant flowering from the base up. The benefits of fan training are really

When fan-training a Shrub rose to grow against the wall as a Climber, as with 'Constance Spry' shown here, it is important to retain as many stems as possible and to start training low down.

two-fold: firstly, this establishes a neat framework from which it is simple to develop a larger plant in subsequent seasons; secondly, it promotes an even, well-balanced spread of growth and flowering. Unfortunately, it is all too common to see bare stems topped by a few flowers in the gutter. I shall suggest how to rectify this on an existing plant, in Problem Solving (page 125).

If you are planting a new Climber, the first thing to do is to wire the wall. The ideal way to do this is to run thick (12-gauge) galvanized wires horizontally along the wall, 18in (45cm) apart, supported by vine eyes every 6ft (2m). It is important that these wires are stretched as tightly as possible, which can be done by using a stick at the end if you are hammering the wires in.

The Climber's shoots should be tied in with thick twine. Never use nylon string, plastic-coated wire twist, or plastic ties; if forgotten, even for one season, they will cut into the growing stems with fatal results. The basic method of tying in is easy and effective. You must first wind the twine twice around the wire, and then tie a knot. The knot will prevent the twine from moving; it will prevent the stem of the Climber rubbing against the wire; and when you wish to remove it at a later date, cutting through a knot will make it easier.

In order to begin your fan, the lowest branches should be tied 12in (30cm) above the ground and nearly parallel with it. Subsequent shoots should be tied in in sequence, without crossing over each other. The Climber can be treated initially almost like a hedge, with the lower side shoots allowed to project further forward than those higher up — in the same way that a hedge is battered. Since the growth will be naturally more vigorous at the top of the stems, this will counterbalance the bottom and help to achieve uniform fullness and flatness when the Climber is in leaf.

A Climber will easily grow up to 4ft (1.2m) or more in a growing season, and when establishing a young rose you should stop and break (pinch out the tip of) any shoot that is growing disproportionately long in relation to the rest of the plant. Never, in any case, allow a rose to grow higher than your ladder will reach, or summer pruning will become very difficult. When growing a Climber under a gutter or window, prune the plant in winter down to at least 18in (45cm) below it or more, depending on the vigour of the variety.

The most precious asset of a Climbing rose is a young shoot that comes from the base. As it develops it should be tied in, regardless of its position, to

The training of Climbing roses is all-important. The first stems should be tied in close to the ground and the twiggy growth should be retained in the centre.

Tying in the stems of Climbing roses as low as possible will result in a magnificent flowering display from the ground upwards.

protect it against wind damage. In the late autumn it can be given its proper place in the sequence, even if this means some untying or removal of older wood. If these shoots occur in the middle of the plant, stop and break some of them 24in (60cm) above the ground, as they can be used more profitably to give flowers lower down.

During the years needed to establish a Climber, it is often worth taking it off the wall and tying it back in, in sequence. When retying, start the fan on one side, move over and do the same on the other side, and finish in the middle. The reason for this is that there is naturally more growth in the middle of the plant where plant's energy is concentrated, so these central stems should be tied in on either side. This sounds like a major undertaking but it is surprisingly easy to do. The result is rewarding; a Climber trained in

this way will be an attractive sight even in the winter months.

As a general rule, Shrub roses, when grown as Climbers, tend to produce more branches, with denser growth than Climbing or Rambling roses. In many ways they are also easier to train, since there will be more stems of equal length to choose from. They should be pruned in exactly the same way as described for their Shrub counterparts (see pages 107-112).

ONCE-FLOWERING CLIMBERS

These, too, should be pruned in the same way as their Shrub counterparts, but before cutting off the vegetative growth in early summer, and again in the autumn, see whether any of the young shoots can be tied in to fill a gap or replace an aging stem to improve the overall framework.

REPEAT-FLOWERING CLIMBERS

Like the Shrubs, these roses require deadheading and summer pruning. It is very important to prevent bare stems at the bottom; most Climbing Tea roses are especially prone to this. To prevent it, try to control the upward growth as much as possible, stopping and breaking strong shoots, and making sure that there is plenty of strong flowering growth at the base. A mature Tea Climber may need thinning out at the top to make it shrub up lower down.

The winter pruning involves reducing all the side shoots to within two or three buds of the main stems, with the exception of the front which is left twiggier and longer, like a Shrub. At this stage any gap should be filled by tying in appropriate shoots.

The exceptions to these rules are the Noisettes like 'Madame Alfred Carrière', 'Desprez à Fleurs Jaunes' and 'Aimée Vibert'. In many respects these roses make a halfway house between Climbers and Ramblers, and are often at their best left unpruned to grow through fruit trees. When grown against a wall they can all too readily become very untidy. However, pruning all the non-flowering shoots just after the first flowering will both encourage a second flush and maintain the neat appearance of the Climber. The pruning of vegetative shoots can and should be repeated as required throughout the season.

During the summer, check that young shoots are not growing up behind the wire, and try your best to ease out any that are. If any shoots are allowed to remain behind the wire, it will be difficult to train the stems in sequence and also they may rub against the wall. If you have a shoot growing behind the wire, wait until the winter, then remove the appropriate wire and thread it back behind the stem.

(above) 'Madame Caroline Testout' is fan-trained on a wall, with all the twiggy growth neatly tied in. Regular deadheading will ensure a succession of flowers throughout the summer.

(left) 'Madame Alfred Carrière' will need to have the non-flowering vegetative growth removed at regular intervals in order to retain a neat overall appearance.

RAMBLING ROSES

Ramblers differ from Climbers in that they have a profusion of very long stems and, with the exception of the Barbier Ramblers, tend to have small flowers held in trusses, which frequently produce attractive hips in the autumn. Many of them, if carefully grown and pruned, can be used in a variety of formal ways in the garden.

RAMBLERS ON ARCHES AND OTHER STRUCTURES

Anyone who has seen the splendour of the arches at Bagatelle and the Roserie de l'Hay-les-Roses outside Paris must wonder how it is done. This dramatic, formal effect is in fact quite easy to achieve; it is a question of choosing the appropriate plant and pruning it as an extension of the way once-flowering shrubs are pruned. Some of the repeat-flowering Shrub roses (see below) can

Arches present a particular problem because of their height. It is essential that you work with a stable ladder in order to do the job properly.

French pruning on arches is achieved by pruning twice during the summer (unless growth is needed to fill a gap) to encourage a dense framework.

During the winter, as much growth as possible is tied in. If increased height is needed, tie in some of the long vegetative 'fishing rods' too.

Ramblers are the best choice for growing on a large arch but strong repeat-flowering Shrub roses can be grown on smaller ones. The rose illustrated in these photographs is 'Tuscany Superb'.

Neatness and shaping are all-important on an arch and all growth needs to be tied.

Correct pruning directs the plant's energy into the balanced production of flowers.

be used on smaller structures, up to 7ft (2m) high and 8ft (2.5m) wide, but for a larger pergola or tunnel only a few varieties of the larger Ramblers will be suitable, such as 'Albéric Barbier' and 'New Dawn'; partially covered structures will be disappointing and will contribute little to an overall design.

It is a false economy to buy a cheap arch or untreated wooden posts, or to erect a larger structure with cheap materials; thin, plastic-coated rods, for example, are no substitute for treated steel. As soon as your rose becomes established, the whole structure will be in danger of collapsing in the first storm, and it is an unenviable task replacing an arch or a pergola under a carefully grown, mature plant.

Structures of this kind provide a far colder and more exposed environment than a wall, and it may take time to get your roses established. It is usual practice to plant equal and opposite, that is to say, to plant the same rose on either side of the structure, even if these opposite pairs change along the length of a tunnel or pergola. When the roses do change, it is a good idea to graduate their colour along the length of the structure.

With such vigorous roses, it is essential to watch out for bare stems at the bottom. When establishing a young plant it is important to stop and break young shoots to achieve twiggy growth at the base of the rose and ensure a balance of flowers all the way up. (If this fails, it is even worth going against all the basic tenets and bending stems downwards or crossways to hide the legginess.) If a rose is allowed to grow to its full height in one season, it will have branches, foliage and flowers that are few and far between. To increase the height once the base is established, take some of the long vegetative shoots that we call 'fishing rods' in the nursery, and tie them in.

Winter pruning of 'Bobbie James' grown on a large arch. Although very vigorous, it is tamed by pruning twice in summer, both early and late in the season.

When training a Rambler on a rope, tie in as many of the vertical shoots as possible in order to create a dense appearance.

This dense framework is reminiscent of a Shrub. The old growth will produce a mass of flowers, as can be seen from the hips in the top photograph.

Filling a gap: you can bend stems downwards and tie them in when this is required to fill a space or an empty-looking area on the structure.

(left) The second summer pruning of 'Brenda Colvin' will direct the plant's energy into the production of atttractive hips as well as ensuring a neat appearance.

At Bagatelle they regularly take the roses off the arches in order to stop and re-tie the lower growth to cover the bare stems at the bottom. It also pays to thin out excess growth from the top at the same time; if this is not done, the rose will gradually thatch, concentrating all its energy into this top growth. If you wish to increase the height of the plant, take some of the autumn fishing rods and tie them in while pruning the rest.

Once the Rambler is established, pruning procedures are as follows: just as the flower buds begin to split and to show colour in early summer, the plant will be covered in long fishing-rod shoots. These are all cut off, leaving the basic structure of the plant. The plant's energy is then directed to the development of flowers. The same procedure is again carried out in late summer, ensuring a good autumn display if it is a hipping variety. There is no need to be anxious about cutting off next season's flowers, for when a fishing rod is cut back it will produce flowers the following season from the next bud down. We have a 'Bobbie James', which is one of the most powerful of all the Ramblers, contained on an arch 8ft (2.5m) high; it has been pruned in this way for the last ten years, and at the height of flowering it is quite difficult to see the leaves for the profusion of flowers.

RAMBLERS ON SWAGS AND PILLARS

Growing roses on swags and up pillars is one of the great French traditions and a good way of dividing a garden: while they give a sense of entering another area, they do not present a formidable barrier. Growing roses in this way is probably one of the most difficult methods to get right. As with most effects, the secret lies in choosing the variety best suited for the work. Good choices are the Barbier Ramblers, creamy-yellow 'Albéric Barbier' and soft pink 'Léontine Gervaise'. 'New Dawn' can be used, but the second crop of flowers tend to be held on long, outward-pointing stems which can destroy the effect. White can be introduced by 'Félicité et Perpétue' or 'Adelaïde d'Orléans'. As a general guide, the pillars

'New Dawn' is grown on a steel tunnel. This will require tight and formal pruning in the French style.

As much of the new growth as possible should be tied in before pruning starts. The shoots on the top of the hoops may need thinning to keep the tunnel in proportion.

Pruning on swags requires the same approach as tunnels and arches, pruning twice during the summer. Avoid the temptation to tie in too much growth. Rambling roses with a naturally pendulous habit are the best choices for swags.

should be 8–10ft (2.5–3m) apart, in order to bear the weight of the swags and the plant, and to survive strong winds. If you are using chains instead of ropes for the swags, cover the chains with sackcloth in order to prevent the rose stems being choked by the chain links as it matures. Whether you plant one variety of rose, or several different varieties, with mixed colours, will depend on how long the structure is, and whether it is a feature on its own or part of a rose garden.

The pruning method is the same as for the Ramblers on arches, above, but with more attention to detail and to overall shape. Two or three of the longest shoots should be kept and tied in to continue the swag, and the basal growth needs to be stopped regularly to ensure that the bases do not become bare-stemmed. However, the number and length o f the stems should be evenly distributed, and the temptation to tie in too much growth should always be avoided.

RAMBLERS ON LOW ROPES

This is an unusual way of enclosing a seat or grass area in the middle of a lawn, or making an edge to a walk. Unlike the taller swags, a wider range of roses can be used, since the density and number of shoots to be tied in is less critical. 'Albertine' and 'New Dawn' can both be used to great effect. An underplanting of a low herbaceous plant like the blue catmint (*Nepeta musinii*) is pretty, and softens the edge.

RAMBLERS TUMBLING OVER WALLS

Those Ramblers which have a naturally pendular habit, like 'Félicité et Perpétue', 'Adelaïde d'Orléans' and 'Wedding Day' – as well as the Barbier Ramblers which will have later flowers in the autumn – are ideal to use for tumbling over walls. It is often more spectacular if you can

'Léontine Gervaise' is seen here tumbling over a low wall to give a cottagey effect. Wires are used to establish the tumbling appearance when the rose is young. Once established, it needs no work apart from deadheading and a little shaping in winter.

plant the rose on the other side of the wall and then tumble it over, instead of planting it in the conventional way by allowing it to grow up and fall back on itself. Ramblers used in this way will need little or no pruning other than tidying for neatness. Wires should be set on the facing side of the wall so that you can pull down and tie in the first long stems, in order to establish the tumbling effect firmly when the rose is young.

RAMBLERS ON BANKS

Ramblers can be grown to tumble down steep banks, though some preparatory work is needed to make the most of this idea. The planting position should be dug as for tree planting (see page 135), to facilitate watering during the first years and to prevent drying out, as slopes are frequently too well drained. A strong square or rectangular wooden frame should be laid on three sides (the fourth side being on the top of the slope) of the planting position around the planting hole, with the top pegged down and resting on the top of the slope, to allow the rose sufficient initial support. Once established, a rose grown in this way should not need pruning.

RAMBLERS GROWN THROUGH TREES

This is a delightful way to grow a Rambler, and curiously does not seem to harm the tree. The rose will need some initial training, with loose string to tie the stems around the tree's trunk, and a few ties on the lowest branches. Alternatively, if the rose is planted at the edge of the trees canopy, it can be trained up a wooden frame and subsequently up a stout rope attached to a branch. After that, it will need little or no pruning, and should be allowed to cascade freely through the top of the tree. The fishing rods will hang down to provide the following season's flowers, and will only need pruning if they are a hazard to anyone passing.

To start the rose we generally prepare a planting hole with fresh soil, lined with an old bucket or large tin with the bottom removed. This then enables the rose to establish without competition from the tree roots and watering is easy and effective. Plant on the south side of the tree, as close to the trunk as possible, allowing for tree roots. With very large trees, because of their thick canopy, it is sometimes better to plant the rose at the outer limit of the branches and let it grow up. Plant the rose outside the drip line of the tree's branches and build a wooden supporting frame for it. The rose might take a couple of seasons before developing a powerful basal shoot, and it is this shoot that should be trained up the outside of the tree. One of the easiest ways to do this is by extending a stout rope from the tree branch down to the supporting frame.

The important thing is to match the size of the Rambler to the size of the tree, and, because most Ramblers have outstanding perfume which is carried well on the wind, to try and site it to catch the prevailing wind.

'Bobbie James' is grown to cascade through a tree, creating an informal, natural effect. It gives an excellent flowering display while requiring little or no pruning.

PRUNING SUMMARY

Early summer:
Prune off all fishing rods down to two or three buds as soon as the calyx splits to show some colour.

Late summer:
Prune back to the flowering height the fishing rods which appear from behind the flowers. Some selected fishing rods may be kept and tied in, either to bring the Rambler to its full height, or to cover up bare stems at the bottom.

Winter:
Prune off all trusses with hips back to the established 'pruning height'. Remove dead wood and snags.

SHRUB ROSES FOR PILLARS AND OBELISKS

The larger repeat-flowering Shrub roses, especially the Bourbons and Hybrid Perpetuals, are well suited for this purpose, and Gallicas such as 'Belle de Crécy' and 'Cardinal de Richelieu' are very good on pillars. You should avoid choosing a variety that is too vigorous for the structure. An obelisk will need only one rose planted in the centre, whereas pillars will probably need one plant on either side. Either way, the rose should be grown up slowly, stopping and breaking the young shoots until a good framework of low twiggy growth is established and tied in. Once you have a good base, the stronger stems can be allowed to grow up.

It is common to see stems corkscrewed around pillars. As a rule this is a mistake – just as the rose gets to the top it will die back to a strong bud lower down the stem, because if the sap is constrained by corkscrewed stems, the plant will select a more logical route (usually the first bud below the corkscrew). They should instead be grown by slowly and regularly pinching out stems to achieve a twiggy and architectural column.

ROSES ON SCREENS

In some positions where a hedge is unsuitable, a screen of roses could be used. If, for example, you wish to hide a neighbouring house without planting along the boundary, you could use a structure of 12ft (3.6m) poles set 8ft (2.5m) apart, with wires running between them at 18in (45cm) intervals. The roses are planted on every pole and tied in along the wires until they have covered the structure; after that they will send cascading branches downwards which should need little or no work.

The two most effective roses for this are 'Adelaïde d'Orléans' and 'Félicité et Perpétue' which, in all but the severest winters, will remain evergreen.

ROSES ON TRELLIS

If a cheap trellis is used, a thick-stemmed and vigorous variety of rose ('Albertine', for example) will grow through the gaps and in a very short period of time split it open. The trellis should be of hard wood or metal (but not wire), and the rose should be chosen carefully. An excellent choice for trellis would be 'Céline Forestier', which has a lot of slender growth and will flower all summer with delightful perfume. Its slender growth means that the rose can be kept mainly on the front of the trellis without becoming a tangled mess.

STANDARD ROSES

There are some very attractive Shrub standards available, like 'Ballerina' and

Roses grown on trellis provide excellent and inexpensive garden dividers. Choose the variety with care, particularly if the trellis is not very sturdy.

'White Pet' ('Little White Pet'). With standard roses, the staking is all-important. Iron poles or scaffold tubes painted black are the least unsightly, and the top of the stake should be level with the point at which the rose is budded. The rose should be tied firmly to the stake at this point, and it is important to tie the standard with a similar knot to the one used for Climbers on a wall (see page 114), to prevent it chafing against the stake. Old tights are excellent for this

purpose as they are very strong and will not graze the wood.

All standards need careful pruning, and this should be done exactly as for the Shrubs, but with closer attention to the shape. The plants should also be protected against winter winds and frosts; in Germany they untie the standard from its support in winter, and bind the stem over like a hoop so that the top can be buried in the ground to avoid the frosts. Given advanced warning of temperatures as low as 10°F (-12°C) or more, this might be worthwhile.

WEEPING STANDARDS

Weeping standards can either be trained downwards over an 'umbrella', or along wires running from the top of the posts to the ground, like a teepee. They should not be pruned during their first two years or they will become too shrubby.

In subsequent years they require practically no pruning, but young shoots should be trained in to fill the gaps. Some roses used in this way, such as 'New Dawn' or 'Albertine', will send out strong upright shoots; these are pruned like fishing rods once the basic shape is established. Gardeners of an earlier age used to tie weights to the top of the stems they wished to keep, so that the standard's appearance was well presented.

It is important that the growth of weeping standard roses is balanced on all sides. Initial training on wires is needed to achieve this effect, then little pruning in subsequent years.

ROSES PEGGED DOWN

This is a rewarding and unusual way of growing a rose. Traditionally, the Hybrid Perpetuals were used: varieties like 'Reine des Violettes' lend themselves well to this method. The idea is to make a half-fan shape of wires from a centre point at the base of the rose. The spokes, usually eight to ten in number and about 5ft (1.5m) long, radiate outwards, and have wires attached with which to peg them down. The rose is allowed to grow unpruned for the first season, then in mid-autumn the shoots are pulled down and tied in sequence, as for a Climber. They will flower down the length of the stem the following summer. In the second year, strong basal growth should be allowed to grow up, and then be tied down, so that the fan is filled. Subsequent maintenance involves pruning for shape as for a Climber, and the occasional replacement of older branches with basal shoots that have appeared during the summer. Dead-heading and summer pruning should be carried out as the variety requires.

ROSES IN POTS

All the China and Polyantha roses do well in pots. If it is possible to remove a bit of patio under the pot, the rose will benefit by being able to extend its roots into the ground. If not, then add some cheap seaweed-based feed to the water every time it is watered. After two or three years, depending on the size of the pot, the rose will become pot-bound. Using a stout pair of gloves, pull the plant out of the pot, and with a hammer or heavy stick bash the rootball until most of the compost has fallen off; then repot it in the same pot, forcing in as much new compost as possible. The Victorian gardeners used a specially shaped piece

(above) This arbour is planted with 'Cerise Bouquet' and 'Woodlands Rambler' (one of our hybrids). Since the arbour is set in a secluded position, away from the formal garden, the pruning is done only lightly, to create a more romantic feel.

of wood to force compost down the side of the pot. This is the trick we use for eight-year-old potted roses that we show at horticultural shows, and it works.

ROSES UNDER GLASS

The greatest problem with roses grown under glass is red spider mite, and unless this is kept firmly under control, roses are not viable as greenhouse plants. A famous rose of Victorian conservatories

(above and below left) Roses in pots need to be watered frequently and repotted in fresh compost every few years. Foliar feed is an excellent form of help for roses restricted by being grown in containers.

was 'Maréchal Niel', a wonderfully scented yellow Noisette. Pruning for roses grown under glass starts at Christmas, as if they were on a wall outside, and provided they are planted in soil and not in a pot, the first crop of roses should appear at Easter. After Easter the glasshouse should be partially shaded. Flowering will continue in flushes, and after the roses have flowered they should be pruned and fed with an organic liquid feed. After flowering, the Victorians used to take the roses down, thin them out and re-tie them. Side shoots were used for the new growth.

Roses grown under glass for cutting need to be side-shooted: the shoots that come from the leaf stalk are removed so that the energy is directed to the flower. They also need to be disbudded (cutting the flower with a long stem is sufficient pruning). Any leaves remaining have the leaf stem partially broken, by splitting it in half at the stem, to encourage bud burst and faster development.

ROSE HEDGES

There are two approaches to hedging with roses. A formal hedge, used as a garden divider or on either side of a path, will usually be made up of a single variety of rose. A perimeter hedge, on the other hand, often uses mixed varieties and has a slightly more untidy habit.

For formal hedging, either once- or repeat-flowering roses can be used. The once-flowerers are ideal for neat work; 'Pompon de Bourgogne' and 'de Meaux' produce low, thick, box-like hedges that need to be pruned back to the flowering height twice in summer. Most Gallicas, like *R. gallica* 'Versicolor' ('Rosa Mundi') and 'Charles de Mills', make excellent hedges provided they are kept in check, as their habit can become lax.

Repeat-flowering roses rapidly lose their shape when the second flush of flowers occurs, and the selection of roses for hedges becomes quite critical when this is taken into account. Polyanthas like 'Yvonne Rabier' and 'Mevrouw Natalie Nypels' are very good for hedges up to 4ft (1.2m), and 'White Pet' for low hedges, to 2ft 6in (75cm). Hedges have to be deadheaded and summer pruned in the same way as individual shrubs, but with the shape of the hedge in mind.

Taller roses like the Hybrid Musks 'Felicia' and 'Moonlight' are also good for hedging. With careful pruning they should flower from the ground upwards, and you should be able to avoid bare stems at the bottom. However, it is difficult to grow a hedge above 5ft (1.5m) without it becoming leggy and bare.

Perimeter hedges do not need so much work or attention and most Rugosas are very effective. Deeply planted, they will rapidly generate the basal shoots which help to thicken the hedge at the bottom and prevent legginess. An attractive hedge can be made from mixing *R. rugosa*

(above) The top of this 'Complicata' hedge has been carefully pruned to round off its top.

(below) 'Felicia' is grown here as a double hedge, complementing the formality of the house.

(above) The appearance of the same hedge when in flower reveals the soft, rounded shaping of the top, which is entirely appropriate here. A more formal effect could be achieved with sharper corners.

'Rubra' and *R. r.* 'Alba', where both the flowers and the hips are of value. Prune with hedge cutters down to 4ft (1.2m), or just above last year's pruning height, in late autumn. Part of the joy of Rugosa hedges is the wonderful golden colour of their autumn leaves.

In general, pruning rules for hedges should follow those specified for the variety chosen. The planting distances depend on the vigour of the variety (the height is usually two-thirds the planting distance). When establishing a rose hedge, do not allow it to reach its eventual height all in one go. The height of the hedge in its first few years should be determined by the lowest plant in the hedge. Like all hedges, they should be battered when they are winter pruned, to form a base that is wider than the top. Since the top is more vigorous, the hedge will be in proportion when the rose is in flower. Battering also keeps the hedge shapely in the event of heavy snow.

PROBLEM SOLVING

*I*t is all very well to describe, as I have done in preceding chapters, how to deal with roses in a perfect situation. However, many of us have to contend with roses which have got out of hand and this chapter is devoted to putting them right. Old roses are virtually indestructible, and you need only follow a few simple rules and have confidence. You will also need long-handled pruners with a parrot-billed cutting blade; secateurs are not strong enough and will make a ragged cut when removing large stems or dead wood. It is unnecessary to apply wound paint; this can inhibit callusing, and the cuts will heal cleanly without it.

ONCE-FLOWERING ROSES

These are out of hand when the bush becomes a sprawling mass of long, floppy growth with few blooms. Your object will be to recreate a dome shape of self-supporting growth, and it is often easier in these circumstances to start pruning from the sides, rather than the top. You will usually find strong shoots coming from the base, with a number of branches coming off them, and you can prune these branches back quite hard, working your way around the bush and gradually upwards. Reduce any remaining shoots in line with the overall shape you require, and gradually reduce the top of the plant in the same way. This will then become the pruning height to which you will prune back in subsequent years.

If the rose has become so leggy that there is no option but to prune it down to thick, bare, woody stems, without any twiggy growth, the rose will produce only vegetative growth the following year. It is vital to stop and break this vegetative growth during the subsequent summer, in order to produce a thick network of flowering growth during the second year.

(left) This rose, R. gallica var. officinalis, has been devastated by a thunderstorm in mid-summer.

(below left) By pruning all the bowed-over branches, the plant regains its shape without affecting its ability to flower the following year.

Establishing a new pruning height can be quite a radical treatment. However, even the oldest wood can regenerate. The best time for this course of action is early winter.

Unlike with Hybrid Teas, it is not necessary to thin out the growth in the middle of Shrub roses. Excess thinning out of the centre will only encourage the outer branches to fall outwards, and as long as the growth is productive it should be kept. However, it is important to remove dead branches whenever they occur, both to prevent disease and to encourage new, stronger growth.

Hybrid Teas can be burnt by frost if pruned too early, but repeat-flowering roses are best pruned in early spring, while Climbing roses can be pruned any time from mid-autumn onwards, once the growth has stopped (and in general, the earlier the better, to avoid wind or snow damage). With the exception of a few varieties (see Proliferation, page 127), we have found over the years that the timing for pruning once-flowering roses makes no difference to flowering times or to the quality of the flowers, while it makes god sense to be able to spread the workload in the garden.

REPEAT-FLOWERING ROSES

This group tends to be quite leggy, with bare stems at the bottom, but they are out of hand when they become so tall and thin that the flowers pull the plants over, or when they are so leggy that the rose's foliage and flowers start 4–5ft (1.2–1.5m) above the ground. You can afford to be quite dramatic with the pruning, cutting the main shoots hard back in early spring, but encouraging any twiggy growth (exactly the growth that should be removed from a Hybrid Tea). Every shoot, including the twiggy growth, will produce a flower, and this growth contributes greatly to the overall appearance of the plant. It is not necessary to thin out the centre of the plant, but if there are new basal shoots it is worthwhile removing some older growth to encourage their development. Outside shoots should be stopped in order to make strong low growth with a healthy crop of flowers.

To stop the rose getting out of hand again, you only need to be firm with the summer pruning. Instead of pruning to the nearest bud below the flowers when deadheading, prune to the lowest bud on the stem. This should be done immediately the flowers are over, otherwise the growth will go to the nearest bud below the blooms. The frequency of deadheading will dictate the continuity; if it is done all in one go the rose will flower not continuously but in flushes.

CLIMBING ROSES

Of all the questions asked about pruning, the majority concern Climbing roses. My reply, that if a Climber has got hopelessly out of hand, the only solution is to take it off the wall and start again, is usually greeted with blank incre-dulity. Yet it is much easier than most people think: all that is required is two people with confidence and a sense of humour. This can be done any time after growth has stopped, from mid-autumn to early spring.

A rose should never be allowed to grow higher than your ladder, or to a height at which you do not feel confident working. So, any growth above this should first be cut off and thinned out. Next, you will have to cut the knots of the string tying the rose to the wires, and probably also remove at least some at least of the wires, as stems will inevitably have grown up behind them. It is at this point that a sense of humour is required, for you will be surrounded by a great tangle of thorny stems lying on the ground. However, rose stems are pliable (especially in late autumn when

(above left) The rose illustrated, 'New Dawn', has been pulled off the wall by a gale.

(left) The growth has been significantly reduced and superfluous growth thinned out. This drastic pruning of the rose will not have an adverse effect on its ability to flower again the following year.

(top right) The Rambler has been replaced on the wall, neatly fanned out.

they have finished growing) and can be dealt with quite firmly. If an important stem does split during untangling, as occasionally happens, you can bind it round with twine, and in most cases this works effectively without lasting damage. The twine will hold it together, allowing the split to heal, and will also keep frosts and disease out of the wound. Modern Climbers (especially Teas) are prone to splitting in this way; their wood is not as strong as it looks.

Your object will be to untangle all the stems so that they can be replaced in sequence from the base, without any of the growth crossing. This counsel of perfection is advocated both for the appearance of the Climber on the wall, and because crossing growth, if not firmly tied in, will rub together. Sometimes, crossed stems cannot be avoided, and they can always be removed later when more appropriate stems have grown in to take their place. The next task is to rewire the wall (see page 97),

and then lay the rose growth out and tie it in in sequence.

The stimulus for growth in a dormant bud is dictated by light and gravity. Even very old stems can regenerate when tied in to lie horizontally, since the energy will be directed to the uppermost buds on the stem. The first stem to be tied in should be as low and horizontal as possible. Any shoots from this stem should be tied in flat against the wall, at a horizontal angle, and if they do not conform to this, should be pruned back to two or three buds and then tied in. The sequence should be followed, with each stem equidistant from the next, and overall priority being given to shape and balance. Even if the end result is only three or four bare stems, it is well worth the effort; the following year will yield plenty of strong new growth. This new growth should be pruned and tied in the following spring and summer to suit the framework already made by the previous year's performance.

Rambling Roses

Ramblers, unlike Climbers, tend to have very dense and vigorous growth, and when a very large Rambler has got quite out of control it would be impossible to take it down and start again. Ramblers are capable of regenerating from even the very oldest wood, and the easiest solution, with a variety like 'Albertine', for example, is to prune it back as hard and flat against the wall as possible in late autumn (extra vine eyes may be needed in strategic places to achieve this).

If you feel it is possible to put a less vigorous rose back into an ordered state, you should drop it off the wall, cut all the stems down to a manageable height, and tie them back in a fan shape. This should be done in the autumn, when the wood has stopped growing. Subsequent strong shoots can be tied in to fill the gaps; these shoots may well be vegetative and not flowering for the first year.

Moving Roses

Most established roses will transplant surprisingly well. Early autumn is the best time to move a rose, for every day in winter when the temperature is over 40°F (4°C), roses will make a surprising amount of root growth, and the more root growth that takes place before the spring, the greater is the rose's chance of survival.

First prune the rose by half, pruning back hard any soft growth, and removing the remaining leaves to avoid any loss of water through transpiration. If the ground is compacted, loosen it first with a fork, but not close to the roots. Then, with a spade, dig a circular trench around the rose, about 18in (45cm) from the base, and two spits deep. Do not worry if you amputate the roots. Next, push the rose over to one side, slice

When moving established roses, first remove the soft growth and leaves that can cause water loss by transpiration. In light soils, staking may be necessary once the rose is in its new position.

through the tap roots, and push it over again on to the opposite side, cutting through any exposed roots with a pair of secateurs until it is free. Shake any soil off the roots as you lift the plant, in case of rose replant sickness; it will anyway root and establish itself far more quickly in fresh new soil. Then cut any ragged root ends with the secateurs, to promote clean calluses which will heal rapidly.

There is an element of luck in this procedure, since the root system can be very one-sided and you can end up with very little root. The amount left will dictate how much more pruning is required. You need to strike a balance between root and top, and this should be approximately half and half – too much top may put the rose under stress when replanting. Any dead snags should be removed as close to the base as possible. The new planting position should be thoroughly prepared (see Planting and Establishing, page 134) and the rose should be planted at least 2in (5cm) deeper than its previous position.

The transplanted rose will need extra feeding to replace the stored energy that has been pruned out. The following spring, if the weather is dry, the rose will need to be watered, with liquid feed incorporated from time to time.

Suckers

The old guide of there being five leaves to a cultivated rose and seven leaves to a sucker does not apply to Old roses since most of them do have seven leaves. Suckers come from the understock onto which the majority of roses are grafted. Twenty years ago most rose growers used *R. canina*, the dog rose, as the understock, which is very prone to suckering. Today, most rose growers, including ourselves, use *R. laxa*, and old garden lore about not hoeing around roses or digging near them for fear of encouraging suckers is no longer relevant. However, suckers do still occur. *R. laxa* is a near relative of the Alba roses and the growth is very similar. The leaves are pale grey-green and the stems pale green with small shark-fin thorns. Suckers are usually produced at some distance from the main stem of the rose in question, but it is important to compare the foliage and thorns of the suspect with those of the main plant, since deep planting regularly produces additional roots from the rose itself, and the sucker may turn out to be a new shoot from the rose.

If it is a sucker, you should excavate as much soil as possible to find out where

If the sucker's growth is entwined in the rose, cut the sucker off and leave it for a day. The dead leaves that result will show the growth which you should cut out.

it originates. If it is close to the surface it can be torn off the root, and this usually prevents its reappearance. If it is too thick to be torn off, the root should, if possible, be cut off with the sucker attached, and dug up. If, however, the sucker is too deep, you may have to dig the whole rose up, saw the sucker off flush with the main root stem, if that is where it is coming from, and replant the rose in a slightly different place because of the risk of rose replant sickness. If none of these solutions is practicable, regular cutting off at ground level will diminish the sucker's vigour.

ROSES NOT FLOWERING

THE NOISETTES

Roses like 'Madame Alfred Carrière', 'Desprez à Fleurs Jaunes' and 'Aimée Vibert' often luxuriate in masses of vegetative growth. Having established the framework of growth in winter, any long fishing rod shoots should be pruned back in summer to two or three buds; this usually tricks the rose into flowering from this point. Any subsequent non-flowering shoots should be pruned in the same way. Over-feeding may also be the problem, and should be stopped.

RAMBLERS

The more powerful Ramblers like 'Kiftsgate' and 'Paul's Himalayan Musk' often take two or three years to flower. The problem arises if they are growing too well, and in these cases feeding and watering should be stopped. An addition of potash in the spring can help to promote flowering growth.

ROTTING BUDS

The usual cause of buds turning brown and rotting is a lack of fertility in the soil, particularly a lack of potash, and,

(above) Summer pruning Noisettes like 'Madame Alfred Carrière' after its first flush of flowers will restore its flowering capacity. The same treatment should be carried out if this rose is grown on a wall.

(above) Rotting buds are caused by a continuous period of rain or a lack of potash in the soil. In either case, deadhead the affected flowers to promote the development of healthy buds.

in young plants, spring drought. Liquid feeding with potash will produce results the following year. Another cause is continuous rain but this does not affect the flowers until they are nearly ready to open. Deadhead the damaged flowers to encourage secondary buds to develop. Sawfly can also cause buds to rot (see Pests and Diseases, page 139).

PROLIFERATION

This disorder is easily recognized by green vegetative growth appearing through the centre of the flower. It seldom affects more than ten per cent of the flowers on a given plant, and then only those of certain varieties: 'Madame Isaac Pereire', 'Variegata di Bologna', some Gallicas and the Climbing form of 'Souvenir de la Malmaison' are particularly vulnerable, and there are occasionally others. It is caused by an early spring followed by a cold period, and there are two solutions. The first is to remove proliferated buds as soon as they appear, so that the plant's energy is diverted to the remaining flowers, and the second is to note down which varieties in your garden are affected, and to leave their pruning until the last possible moment in late spring.

DIEBACK

If a stem, or more than one stem, on a healthy, flowering rose dies back, this is not uncommon and is no cause for alarm. It may simply be caused by physical damage from frost, but you should always check for signs of stem canker (see Pests and Diseases, page 138). Cut out the affected stem at ground level.

Do not be alarmed if proliferation occurs: it is caused by cold weather in late spring and can be resolved by removing the remaining buds as soon as they appear and by delaying spring pruning.

THE SOIL

The condition and make-up of your soil will to a great extent determine what plants you can grow, and how well they will flourish. In general, roses prefer light soils to heavy clay soils. A light, open soil will have better drainage, will encourage the development of fibrous root systems, and will allow the rapid exchange of plant foods. Heavy soils will need lightening with gravel and sand to improve drainage and aeration, and also to reduce the risk of waterlogging. However, most Old roses, particularly the once-flowering varieties and the Rugosas, will thrive in most soil types. As a simple guide, if you have dog roses growing in your local hedgerows, Old roses will grow in your garden.

The further south you go in continental Europe, and thence to north Africa, the lighter the soil becomes, and the better the roses flourish. In Arusha in Tanzania, at a height of 4,000ft (1,200m), there is a rose farm where the roses thrive in volcanic tufa. However, some very light sandy soils may present problems because they quickly lose minerals; where this is the case it is wiser to use strong, once-flowering roses.

COMPOST AND ORGANIC MANURES

The addition of plenty of organic matter undoubtedly produces the most successful results with roses, and organic gardening in general suits them better than short-term artificial fertilizers. Organic matter is broken down by air-breathing bacteria in the top layer of soil (the humus), and feeding these bacteria with a good supply of compost will ensurethat there is sufficient food for the plants. Having gone to considerable lengths to establish a thick layer of humus, we now never dig our own garden; the soil is constantly improved and aerated by the

(opposite) Laying out a small formal rose garden: note the generous path widths.

(left) Preparation is the most important part of planting. This involves the elimination of perennial weeds, thorough digging and the addition of lavish quantities of well-rotted organic matter.

(above) A compost heap will provide the ideal organic mater to incorporate in the soil. Turn it over with a fork before adding it to your beds.

(above) A rose established on its own roots will have a quantity of fine, hair-like roots which take in the nutrients in the soil.

Quality of foliage is always a good indication of a fertile soil. The speed and energy of the photosynthesis process will ensure flowers of an equal quality.

action of earthworms. We prefer to mulch with compost in late summer rather than the traditional way in spring, spreading it after the summer pruning. The compost is thus broken down sufficiently to give the roses the stored energy they need to go through the winter and start growing again in the spring. On any winter day when the temperature is over 40°F (4°C) there will be root growth, and it therefore makes sense to provide the food in advance.

Even the smallest of gardens can have a compost heap. The more varied the ingredients, the greater its value, and the trick is to add these ingredients to the compost heap and not directly to the rose. Start with garden refuse, such as soft prunings, grass cuttings and any deciduous leaves, then add suitable domestic refuse, for example vegetable peelings, fruit skins and eggshells. (but do not add meat or other proteins because of rats). The occasional bag of manure is a bonus, as is wood ash or ash from a bonfire, since the potash it contains is less likely than a chemical formula to leach through the compost. Dried blood or hoof and horn are also valuable additions.

Farmyard manure should be used sparingly round roses, and then only when it is black and crumbles easily; fresh manure may burn the roots or stems of young plants. Birds love manure, and large lumps will be turned over by blackbirds until they dry out and lose any value. Shred well-rotted manure with a spade in the barrow before spreading it, and it will quickly be incorporated in the humus; a covering of wood ash will help to prevent the birds from finding it. As in the case of mulching with compost, it is best to add manure in late summer after pruning, but on light soils it is worth doing in the spring as well.

Spent mushroom compost is not in itself of great use. The mushrooms will have extracted the value from the compost, and it is usually sterilized before delivery. However, when mixed with grass cuttings and manure (bagged or from the farm), it provides a useful short cut to establishing a good humus. It is also excellent as an ingredient in the compost heap. Peat and peat-substitutes are of no value to roses at all.

FERTILIZERS

The idea that all roses require chemical fertilizers is deeply ingrained in us. Contrary to popular belief, Old roses in general do not. What they do need is a good, light soil and plenty of compost. Unless you know that there is a specific mineral deficiency, chemicals should be avoided. The indiscriminate use of artificial fertilizers is undesirable for two reasons. Firstly, it may well reduce the rose's resistance to disease, and secondly, the excessive or repeated use of nitrogen can cause a build-up of salts in the soil and therefore in the plants. This is known as the EC or electrolysis count, and it adversely affects osmosis — the process by which food is distributed to all the cells of the plant.

Where specific deficiencies in the soil do need to be corrected, chemical fertilizers (which may be either organic, like liquid seaweed, or inorganic) are of great value to the gardener. The trace elements iron and manganese, for example, are 'locked up' in chalky or limy soil, and inaccessible to plants unless released by the addition of the chemical sequestrol. Roses tend not to show overt symptoms of mineral deficiency, but poor growth or susceptibility to disease, especially on chalky soil, may be caused by a deficiency of this kind, and these essential trace elements can be made accessible if they are chelated (or sequestered) artificially.

It is usually more effective to apply a liquid fertilizer through the foliage than by pouring it in at the roots of a plant, and on a very light sandy soil, or in difficult pH conditions, foliar feeding can be especially beneficial. In order to avoid the problems associated with an excessive use of such fertilizers, we normally apply foliar feed only once during the year, in late spring.

Good soil and the correct use of any fertilizers needed will create a wonderful display on this arch (shown here in late spring just before the roses flower). Tight and detailed pruning will also ensure the attractive appearance of a rose arch.

The rose arch in full flower. 'Tuscany Superb' reveals the benefits reaped from good soil preparation.

CHEMISTRY OF THE SOIL

The soil's chemistry depend to a large extent on the balance of the three main elements in the soil, and an understanding of the basic composition of the soil is helpful in deciding whether there are any mineral deficiencies and what, if any, treatment is required.

The three main elements are nitrogen (N), phosphorus (P) and potassium (K), and a balance between these interacting elements is needed for the health of all plants. The acidity or alkalinity of your soil (the pH) will affect this balance, so it is important to establish what the level is. For example, acid soils may be deficient in phosphorus; alkaline ones in potassium; and an excess of one element can lead to deficiencies in the others In a neutral soil, phosphorus and potassium tend to leach out at a slower rate than nitrogen, thus creating an imbalance and a shortage of nitrogen. The acidity or alkalinity of the soil also affects the availability of some other nutrients, and if roses are to be grown on either very acid or very alkaline soils, some extra work will be needed to provide them with the balance that suits them best.

(above) The different shades of green and the variety of leaf shapes are full of interest. The roses have been planted and pruned so that they just touch each other when in flower, with space left for companion planting. This will eliminate most weeds.

(left) During the summer months it is best to correct mineral imbalances by the use of foliar feeds. In winter, lime can be added directly to the soil.

To establish whether your soil is acid, alkaline or neutral, talk to local farmers or nurserymen, or use a soil testing kit, readily obtainable from any garden centre, to determine the pH reading. A neutral (i.e. balanced) soil will have a reading of 7.0. Anything above this will be on the alkaline side; anything below on the acid. Roses like a pH of 5.5 to 6. Few people are fortunate enough to have the ideal pH, but plenty of organic matter, preferably garden compost, coupled with an occasional foliar feed, will normally help to correct any imbalance. Once you have determined your soil's composition, you will be able to choose an appropriate liquid fertilizer if you feel this is necessary to compensate for any deficiencies. It is important to use an NPK fertilizer even if you are treating a deficiency in one element only: the numbers on the bottle will indicate the ratio of elements included. A general fertilizer is rated at 8: 4: 4, to allow for the faster leaching out of nitrogen; a fertilizer high in potassium reads 4: 4: 8.

NITROGEN

Nitrogen is quickly leached through the soil and is therefore the most common deficiency. Because of the way bacteria release minerals, the addition of garden compost is the best way to provide a steady supply of nitrogen, whereas artificial applications are quickly lost, and may encourage fungal diseases. If compost is not available, use a slow-release fertilizer with an NPK formula.

PHOSPHORUS

Phosphorus deficiency may be a problem on acid soils. In mid-spring, apply either an NPK fertilizer with a high P number, or superphosphates alone, but only when a deficiency is established.

POTASSIUM

Potassium deficiency is often a problem on light, sandy soils and chalk. Apply an NPK fertilizer with a high K number, or sulphate of potash, in mid-spring.

CALCIUM

Calcium deficiency often occurs in acid soil or a light, sandy soil, and is the reason why farmers lime the fields. Most soil testing kits will indicate how much lime is needed to raise the pH of your soil. This is usually applied in winter.

MAGNESIUM

Magnesium deficiency is usually associated with a deficiency in calcium. By correcting the calcium deficiency, sufficient magnesium will be added.

ROSES UNDER STRESS

Quite often a rose will start to weaken because of lack of food, but it is possible to revive even well-established plants organically. Because today's roses are budded onto *R. laxa* understock, and these very rarely produce suckers, we can use techniques that older generations dared not; rose roots occupy a surprisingly small area, and it is perfectly safe to dig quite close to them. If you dig a circular trench about a spade's width (9in/23cm) around the rose, you can then fill it with compost or manure to provide the extra food the plant needs. Any cut roots will quickly callus without harm, and the surplus soil can be jacketed around the base of the rose.

SPECIFIC REPLANT DISEASE

Whenever a new rose is planted in the same position as another rose which has grown there for more than two years, the problem of 'rose replant sickness' can occur. The probable causes are that

(left) The roses on the right-hand side of this arch are growing less well than those on the left, grown with climbing companions, including honeysuckle and vines, which protect the roses in hot weather.

(above) All the roses in this bed are showing signs of rose replant sickness. This is caused by monoculture (growing nothing but roses in a bed). The disease can be rectified but it is often easier to re-site the bed.

the fertility of the soil has become locked up, due to a mineral deficiency created by the previous rose, and that there is a build-up of harmful micro-organisms in the soil. It shows itself in very feeble growth, a general lack of vigour, distorted, if any, flowers, and susceptibility to disease. If this is the case, the rose should be removed and then destroyed.

In order to prevent the occurence of rose replant sickness, the risk can be reduced in three ways before a new rose is planted. First, the soil can be sterilized with a proprietary soil sterilizer. Secondly, the fertility of the soil can be improved. Thirdly (the old-fashioned solution, which is still the best), as much of the soil as possible can be replaced from a fresh source, and plenty of organic matter added. These solutions are feasible in the case of a single specimen, but are harder to carry out where a complete bed is affected. It is possible to re-make a whole bed, but it may be better to grass the area over and create a new one.

(above) Roses under stress through lack of nutrients and poor drainage of the soil.

(right) 'Kiftsgate' growing wild by the side of a stream will always have sufficient moisture.

IRRIGATION

We never water the soil around our established roses, or indeed the garden in general. Surface irrigation encourages the production of shallow root systems that are dependent on further artificial watering. In the event of a dry summer resulting in a hosepipe ban, irrigated plants will suffer more than those which have developed a root system that taps the natural water level in the soil. Watering can also encourage very soft growth which then becomes a target of disease. Furthermore, frequent watering causes minerals and plant food to leach out from the soil.

The most important plants to irrigate are newly planted roses, to help them establish, as well as Climbers and Ramblers planted against walls, below which the soil may be dry. Soil at the foot of walls is often dry because the foundations absorb moisture from the ground. Even with established Climbing roses, it is worth making a hole with a crow bar, during the winter, at the base

of the rose to a depth of 18in (45cm). This is then lined with plastic pipe, cut off at soil level and plugged. During the summer water can be trickled down the pipe with some liquid feed diluted in it. In any situation where watering has to be done, it is worth adding a liquid seaweed fertilizer to replenish the minerals which will have leached out.

In southern Italy, where summer droughts are common, roses are pruned quite hard in early summer, after flowering. They can then endure the heat and dryness of summer without stress. Early in the autumn the repeat-flowering varieties burst into flower once again, their summer rest apparently as beneficial to them as our winter one.

Planting and Establishing

The best time to plant Old roses is in late autumn to early winter, unless you suffer from very cold winters. Every day the air temperature is over 40°F (4°C) there will be some root growth, which should mean that the rose is well established by the time spring arrives.

Old roses grafted (budded) onto *R. laxa* rootstock provide the best quality plants. Bare-rooted roses are the best choice (remember to order them in the summer for autumn delivery, or for spring delivery if your winters are harsh); container-grown roses are equally good but will require more watering and attention to start with. Some nurseries offer roses as rooted cuttings, but these are not good value; the roots will be fine and shallow and prone to frost and drought; as a result they will be significantly slower to establish. The same is true of micro-propagated plants.

Planting is easy, provided the preparation has been done first. The old adage of what you put in, you get out is certainly true for roses. Roses need to be given the best possible conditions, especially in difficult soils. Essentially, this means organic matter: quantities of well-rotted farmyard manure and garden compost (but not peat) should be incorporated into the planting position. Beware of fresh manure, whether from the farmyard or bagged, which has a very high nitrogen content and can easily burn the roots or stems of a young rose; only use manure when it is black and crumbles easily. Roses, contrary to popular belief, prefer light soils; heavy soils will need to have gravel and sand added to the organic matter to improve drainage.

It is tempting to prepare a planting position several weeks in advance. However, soil structure is quite fragile and the drainage can go wrong if a hole is dug and then left open for several weeks. It is better either to carry out the

The rose which has been deeply planted is seen to be producing more basal shoots than its more shallowly planted neighbour.

preparation and refill the hole, or to do the work on the day that you intend to plant your rose.

If a bed is to be cut out of a lawn, you can do one of two things. You can cover the whole area with 6in (15cm) of manure and leave it for six weeks to rot down the turf, then remove the manure, digging and trenching both it and the rotted-down turf into the new bed. Or you can shave off the turf and dig and then prepare individual planting positions. Decaying turf will need a top dressing of nitrogen in order to help the bacteria break it down.

Preparing a Planting Position

To prepare a planting position for a bare-rooted rose, dig out a hole about 12in (30cm) wide, to a depth of one and a half spits (one and a half times the length of the spade's blade). Break up the bottom

of the hole with a fork, then add organic matter or an organic concentrate, shredding solid matter with a spade first, and mixing it with some soil. Place the plant gently in the hole to check that the hole is deep enough.

Old roses differ from their modern counterparts in the depth at which they should be planted. Because modern roses of the 1920s were weaker than the understock, the practice was to plant with the point of union (that is, where the stems and roots meet) at the surface of the soil. Old roses, however, should be planted with the point of union at least 1in (2.5cm) below the soil surface, when they will rapidly establish their own roots around the understock. Planting like this will prevent windrock, which is a common cause of roses dying, and when the understock eventually dies out, the young shoots from the rose's own roots will take over. Check, however, that these are genuine shoots and are not suckers (see Problem Solving, page 126).

Once the hole is prepared, and if necessary watered, spread the roots out lightly and replace the soil, stopping to firm it in every 6in (15cm) so as to avoid air pockets. Make sure that the union is at the right depth, and when the rose is finally firmed in, add a top dressing of pelleted chicken manure or blood, fish and bonemeal, and water in. Freshly dug soil will inevitably subside, so you may need to bring in more soil later to maintain the correct depth of planting. In heavy soils it is important to avoid stamping in young plants with hobnail boots; this will compact the soil which, in spring, will set like concrete.

Container-grown roses are planted in the same way as bare-rooted roses, but the finished hole should be the same size as the container. Water the hole, then turn the container upside down and tap it against the spade handle; if the compost comes away from the roots, plant rose and compost in the hole, water again and cover with a layer of soil.

Roses grown under trees, next to hedges or free-standing in grass, require a different approach. When digging out the planting hole, line it with an old bucket or large can with the bottom removed, fill it with fresh soil and organic matter, and plant the rose. This will prevent grass or tree roots from taking the goodness or moisture from the soil round the young rose, and makes watering in dry spells easy. It will also facilitate weed control. This is important, as the basal growth of roses can be inhibited if weeds or grass are allowed to take too firm a hold.

Young roses will need to be watered, especially in dry spells in early summer. However, irrigation of any type causes minerals and plant food to leach out of the soil, so the addition of a liquid seaweed fertilizer, or any similar preparation, will help to establish good growth. Roses grown against walls may also suffer from lack of water – either because the wall itself absorbs what moisture there is, or because the rose's roots are in a 'rain shadow' at the foot of the wall. Always plant the rose at least 18in (45cm) away from the wall, and train the shoots towards it. You can also insert a vertical length of plumbing pipe from the base of the planting hole to the surface of the soil, with a bung in the top. This will allow you to trickle water directly to the roots as needed. Even well-established Climbers will benefit from this; use a crowbar, when the soil is wet, to make a hole for the pipe.

When digging a hole for a container-grown rose, make the hole slightly deeper than the container itself, then rake in a quantity of organic matter.

Water the hole thoroughly before planting the rose. Lift the rose, with its rootball and the soil surrounding it, on a spade and lower it gently into the hole.

Once the rose is in place, lightly firm the soil around it, making sure the rose is deeply planted.

PESTS AND DISEASES

After reading this section, you may be inclined never to touch roses again. But remember that as commercial rose growers we simply cannot allow disease in our garden – it would be bad for business! So we tend to err on the pessimistic side in order to avoid possible problems. I am often asked about the organic control of disease. While the methods of control that we use are not strictly 'organic', neither are they harmful to plants, insects (other than greenfly or whitefly) or the environment.

Until the 1960s, disease resistance was not a serious consideration in the breeding of roses. Thereafter, air pollution control and smokeless zones contributed significantly to the reduction of sulphur in the atmosphere and as a result there was a marked increase in the fungal diseases that affect roses. More recently, there has been evidence to link this increase to the widespread use of artificial nitrogenous fertilizers. There is also a possible link between the repeat-flowering China gene and susceptibility to disease, although the Old roses and repeat-flowering hybrids raised during the nineteenth century are much less prone to disease than their modern counterparts. As a result, many garden designers today are specifying the use of these older varieties.

Diseases are also on the increase as a result of the agricultural policy of set-aside. Rust and mildew occur naturally in grasses, and if the grass is not sprayed or cropped, airborne spores multiply and drift into our gardens.

Disease is minimized if a plant is healthy. It will be less resistant to disease if it is under stress from lack of nourishment or from drought, and it will also be a target for disease if it is producing very soft growth as a result of over-feeding or over-watering. Good garden hygiene plays an important part in the prevention of disease. After pruning, you should take care to rake up all the leaves. In mild winters, when leaves may hang on until late spring, these are often a source of fresh infection, so where varieties are especially susceptible to blackspot or rust it is worthwhile removing the old leaves by hand. Over the years we have found that a particular plant may often be the culprit in introducing disease to the garden. This is noticeably the case with blackspot, and in severe cases the plant may simply have to be dug up and burned. All roses in the garden should also be doused with a winter wash of disinfectant.

1. Mildew
2. Blackspot
3. Leaf hopper damage
4. Iron deficiency (chlorosis)
5. Leaf scorch
6. Herbicidal damage
7. Sawfly damage
8. Rust
9. Rust (underside of leaf)

SPRAYING

It is important to prevent disease spores from becoming established on a plant, and we start spraying as soon as the shoots start to open and show young leaves. We then spray every fortnight, alternating the chemicals to achieve as wide a control as possible. The success of spraying depends on starting early and doing it regularly and frequently. You should avoid spraying in full sun, which may result in leaf scorch, and on windy days, when you may get more on yourself than the roses. We first use a spray containing an aphicide that is harmless to other insects, and follow this with one directed against rust. If we find disease taking a hold, we use a double strength solution, but this should not be done more than twice a year.

When spraying roses, the spray should be adjusted to produce fine droplets in a medium spread. It is important to maintain pressure to produce an even distribution. There is no need to soak the plant; too much will leave droplets of white chemical on the leaves. But it is important, especially with rust, to spray underneath the leaves. Climbers should be sprayed from a step ladder or from an upstairs window. If the rose leaves are given a fine dusting of spray it is surprising just how quickly the job can be completed.

FUNGAL DISEASES

Every year a different weather pattern will favour a different disease. A warm, moist summer can produce a lot of blackspot, and a dry, airless summer may result in mildew. Early and frequent spraying is the most effective prevention, as is a winter wash and the avoidance of artificial fertilizers. By the time the disease is visible the plant will have been affected, but regular examination of the foliage for signs of the disease in its early stages still pays off by enabling you to tackle it earlier.

MILDEW

Mildew (powdery mildew) tends to thrive in dry, airless conditions, and usually from mid-summer onwards. Because it is late in appearing, you can achieve considerable preventive control by starting to spray early. However, some varieties of rose, like 'Raubritter' and 'Dorothy Perkins', are so prone to mildew that they are hardly worth growing, and I do not include them in this

Powdery mildew is one of the more familiar diseases affecting roses. Mildew develops on the leaves, stems and buds, which may fail to open, while the leaves can wither and drop prematurely.

Rust is distinguished by orange spots on the leaves, which then turn black. If left untreated, it can defoliate the whole plant. Rust spores survive the winter, so any fallen rose leaves should be collected in autumn and burned.

book. Mildew attacks the young growth of *R. gallica* 'Versicolor' ('Rosa Mundi'), *R. gallica* var. *officinalis*, and some other once-flowering roses, but only at the end of the summer when this growth will anyway be shortly removed by the summer pruning regime.

RUST

Rust is the earliest of the fungal diseases to develop. Spores are over-wintered in the black pustules left on fallen leaves, and these, spread by wind or rain, quickly reinfect the plant. By the time you see the tell-tale signs – orange spots on the leaves – the plant will be quite heavily infected. We have had more cases of rust in the nursery than of any other disease, and it seems to affect varieties that were not previously susceptible. Scientific evidence has proved the link between fertilizers and the increased incidence of rust, so if you have rust in the garden, you should avoid giving the affected plant any form of fertilizer or even manure.

Winter washing will reduce the likelihood of rust, as will good garden hygiene, and there are several proprietary products on the market which will control and quite quickly eliminate this particular problem.

Blackspot can be distinguished from leaf scorch (caused by spray damage) by its irregular pattern and the size of the blotches.

BLACKSPOT

Blackspot tends to affect the repeat-flowering roses, probably because of the predominance of the China gene. It has the ability to over-winter on the stems, so winter washing is of special importance when tackling the disease. Hard pruning will remove a lot of over-wintering spores, and it is always worth raking off infected leaves in the late autumn to prevent the disease transferring to the stems. If they are removed earlier than this, new shoots may be encouraged to emerge, which will then be at risk from frost.

CANKER

Canker in various forms may affect the 'die-backs' on the young stems of roses in wet weather. They are of little consequence provided they are removed as part of the general maintenance. Stem canker, however, is more serious. It is caused by a fungus infecting a wound, and the area around it will turn brown and peel back. Once a stem is girdled in this way, the growth above will die. The only effective treatment is to prune down below the canker to help new growth. If the problem persists it is better to dig the plant up and burn it. One of the few Old roses to suffer is 'Boule de Neige', but if deeply planted it seems to regenerate almost in proportion to the infection. Canker does not appear to transfer to other plants.

Canker lesion on a young rose stem.

VIRUS

Rose mosaic virus is rarely found in the garden because most rose nurseries require phytosanitary certificates from the Ministry of Agriculture, and if their inspectors find the disease the offending plants will be dug up and burned. The symptoms are a yellow mosaic pattern on very pale leaves, affecting most of the mature leaves of a plant. The diamond shape of the mosaic distinguishes the virus from any mineral deficiency that may show similar colouring. The way the virus is transmitted is not known, though aphids are suspected, but there is no cure and the only sensible course is to destroy the plant.

The main symptom of rose mosaic virus is a yellow diamond pattern on pale leaves. Plants showing this symptom should be destroyed.

INSECT PESTS

A number of insects attack Old roses but, apart from greenfly, these rarely pose a serious threat to the gardener.

APHIDS

Aphids should be controlled as a possible source of rose mosaic virus, and because the honeydew can be a source of bacteria and fungal infection. There are proprietary sprays against aphids that contain specific aphicides and will not harm other insects. Used as part of the regular spraying programme, these will contain and control the seven varieties of aphid (chiefly, greenfly and blackfly) that attack roses, but if they get out of control you may need to give an additional spray.

Aphids are commonly found feeding in large colonies. These very small green, pink, or black insects appear in spring, with winged and wingless forms grouped around young rose buds and stems.

RED SPIDER MITE

Red spider mite is a serious pest on roses grown under glass, as they thrive in dry, warm conditions. In exceptional summers they may become established on Climbers grown outdoors, but this is rare. Regular misting with water helps, as they dislike moist conditions, and there are proprietary sprays available. Probably the best solution in the glasshouse is to use red spider mite predators which can be acquired commercially.

Red spider mite, shown greatly enlarged, with the typical signs of infestation on a rose leaf.

ROSE LEAF HOPPER

Rose leaf hopper is revealed by lots of white spots on the foliage of Climbing roses. When disturbed, a mass of white-fly-like insects fly out. The effects are unsightly rather than harmful, unless they multiply out of hand in a dry summer. It is important to spray an appropriate insecticide under the leaves.

Rose leaf hoppers – white, jumping, winged bugs – cause white spots on the leaves of Climbers.

SAWFLIES

Sawflies have egg-laying organs with a serrated edge with which they make cuts to deposit their eggs. Some have caterpillar-like grubs which eat the leaves or turn them into skeletons. Sometimes they will eat one side of the leaf only, leaving quite large irregular blisters on the other. The females lay their eggs in the young shoots, often those with flower buds, which then turn brown and shrivel; these should be removed as soon as they are noticed, to prevent the eggs from hatching out. The females of the second type lay eggs on the rose leaves, which then curl up. They will try out a number of leaves before selecting one on which to lay, but all those leaves will curl. The sawfly pupate or over-winter as larvae in the soil under the rose; a good hoeing will help to reduce their numbers effectively.

Banded sawfly over-winter in snags, and their presence can be seen when the snag has a hole in the centre. Occasionally in mid-summer they will burrow down healthy growth, causing the stem to swell and the leaves to curl. Snags should be removed as part of the winter pruning. Any good systemic insecticide will control sawfly.

(top) Sawfly larvae feeding on the upper surface of a rose leaf, showing the characteristic transparent 'windows' caused by eating away the surface tissues.

(middle) Rose stem showing the severe damage caused by the female leaf-rolling rose sawfly.

(below) The magnified larva of a leaf-rolling rose sawfly showing damage to the foliage.

(above and right) The leaf cutter bee (shown here in flight) cuts circular fragments from leaves, which are then used to line the cells in which they rear their young.

FRIEND NOT FOE!

Virtually everybody is familiar with the ladybird, and any gardener will tell you that they are welcome in our gardens with their voracious appetite for harmful aphids. Ladybirds come in a variety of sizes and colours, with any number of spots – from the common 7-spot (shown below), to the yellow 22-spot, or black 2-spot, where the spots are red in colour, the opposite of that shown below.

Perhaps less familiar are the ladybird larvae – very different in appearance from the adult and equally fond of aphids. They can often be seen feeding in groups (see below) and should be made to feel as welcome as the adults!

POLLEN BEETLES

These small black, flea-like beetles, which occur in mid-summer, are free-flying and cannot be controlled. They have become a particular nuisance in areas of the countryside where oil-seed rape is grown. Pick roses grown for cut flowers before the flowers open.

HERBICIDE DAMAGE

Roses are very sensitive to herbicides. The most frequent cause of death or of feeble growth in a rose is the use of a

(above) Herbicide damage is distinguished by the young growth becoming thin and twisted.

---

nearby weed suppressor. The chemicals that suppress weed germination accumulate in the soil and inhibit the rose root system, so unless you have an invasion of ground elder or bindweed, you should avoid using them. When roses are planted near paths, special care should be taken to avoid chemicals spreading into the soil. If you must use them, put a hood over the sprayer, keep the pressure low, and wait for a windless day, since even the vapour is enough to etiolate the rose foliage.

ANIMALS

MOLES

Moles denote the presence of earthworms and fertile soil, so it is encouraging in some ways to see them at work. However, they are also very destructive; their tunnelling can affect plant roots, especially those of young roses, and cause drying out of the soil.

RABBITS

Rabbits do not like once-flowering Old roses because of the balsam-like smell of the foliage. However, any rose with China ancestry will be attacked immediately. Portland Damasks and Perpetual Mosses are not usually much affected, but a hard winter will prompt rabbits to attack any rose. Their presence is revealed by scarring on the base of the plant, and new shoots chewed right down. You must do all you can to ensure that rabbits cannot enter your garden, using chicken wire to fill in any gaps at the base of fences or hedges.

DEER

Deer can quickly destroy an entire garden; their effect is devastating, and only Moss roses will be left untouched. If deer are a problem in your area, erect high fencing round the garden's perimeter.

MAINTENANCE CALENDAR

Winter Continue pruning Shrub roses. As the hips fall off, prune both Shrubs and Ramblers. Winter-wash any roses that have been infected with fungal disease. Spread well-rotted compost, manure or wood ash, if available, around the roses.

Early Spring Start to prune repeat-flowering Shrub roses back to the previous year's pruning height. Rake up any fallen rose leaves and remove any leaves that have overwintered on the plants.

Mid-Spring Spray with fungicide and aphicide (these can be mixed together) as soon as the buds break. Follow this up two weeks later with a different fungicide. Correct any mineral deficiencies.

Late Spring Continue the spray programme. Watch out for dry spells with young roses and water if necessary.

Early Summer Prune the vegetative shoots on once-flowering Shrub roses as soon as the calyx splits. Remove non-flowering shoots (known as fishing rods) on Ramblers and once-flowering Climbers. Start deadheading roses in flower and watch out for proliferation (green centres) on susceptible varieties.

Late Summer Prune the vegetative shoots again and tidy up any non-hipping once-flowering varieties. Stop deadheading repeat-flowering roses. Spread well-rotted compost or manure around the roses. Keep spraying any varieties still showing disease and note these for winter washing.

Early Winter Transplant any roses which need to be moved. Start pruning Climbers and Ramblers, leaving any varieties with hips for later in the winter. Start pruning once-flowering Shrubs as the weather permits, especially if the roses are underplanted with bulbs or early spring flowers.

INDEX

AUTHOR'S ACKNOWLEDGMENTS

I am very grateful to the many people who have made this book what it is and enabled me to find the time to write it while continuing to run our busy nursery.

Gardening with Old Roses would be nothing without its photographs and illustrations and Teresa's evocative photography was a source of inspiration as the book developed. She has an excellent knowledge of roses and captured them on film when they were at their finest. Teresa travelled with me throughout England and Scotland and, much further afield, to Turkey, often getting up before dawn to catch the early morning light. I feel the book is made by its photographs and I am deeply grateful for her dedication and artistry. My son John took the photograph of 'Baron Girod de l'Ain' on page 79 and I thank him for allowing me to include it. I am also grateful to Marion Nickig for letting us reproduce her photograph of Teresa and me on the back flap of the jacket.

I am extremely indebted to my brother-in-law, Simon Buckingham, for his delightful illustrations of rose gardens, which capture the timeless and romantic atmosphere associated with Old Roses.

Here at Cottage Garden Roses, I would like to thank Paul Edwards for all his hard work at the nursery, allowing me the time to write. Baden Fergusson has helped greatly with the hybridizing of Old Roses and I am honoured to be able to introduce two new varieties, 'Kirsten Klein' and 'Teresa Scarman'. I am sure his work with the musk roses in the form of Devon Musks will produce excellent

results in years to come. Richard McCausland was very helpful in preparing the pruning stages of Old Roses for photography and assisted me with this pruning section of the book.

One of the rewarding things about writing a book is the kindness and help which so many people extend. The generous people in the following list allowed us to photograph in their gardens and I would like to convey my gratitude for this:

Mr and Mrs C. Dumbell, Sir Hardy Amies, Mrs J. Stevens, Mr and Mrs J. Gough, Mrs B. Gilmour, Lord and Lady Pym, Mr and Mrs B. Brolly, Mr and Mrs A. Monckton, Mr and Mrs J. Hill, Lord Saye and Seal, Sir Richard and Lady Lloyd, Mr and Mrs Compton, Mr and Mrs S. Hopkinson, Mrs K. Waddell, Mrs P. Harmer, Mr and Mrs E. Sherman, Lord and Lady Scarman, Mrs S. Swallow, Mrs A. Huntingdon, Mr and Mrs M. Lane-Fox, Mr and Mrs R. Fox, Mrs P. Afia and Mrs Rosemary Verey.

We were treated with great hospitality during our visit to Turkey and I would like to extend my appreciation to: Resul Taztan, Durnus Erkorknaz, Rahmi Babaraz, Mustafa Gokiek, Hasan Kigukberber, Yusuf Aydin.

Finally, but not least, my special thanks to the team at HarperCollins, in particular Carole McGlynn for her editing, Amzie Viladot for the design, and Polly Powell for commissioning the book. I am also indebted to Caroline Taylor for the constructive and helpful points she raised as an independent copy editor.

OLD ROSES BY MAIL ORDER

The following nurseries stock the varieties of Old Roses described in the book. They all operate a mail order service:

Cottage Garden Roses
Woodlands House
Stretton
near Stafford ST19 9LG
Tel. 01785 840217
Fax 01902 850193

Roses du Temps Passé
Agents in Europe:

Italy
Vivaio, Anna Peyron
Fraz. S. Genesio
10090 Castagneto Po (To)
Tel. 011-912982

Belgium
Daniel Schmitz Horticulture
Bellevaux 19a
4960 Malmedy
Tel. 080/33.75.34

Germany
Lacon GmbH
6832 Hockenheim
J.S. Piazolostrasse 4a
Tel. 010 496 205 4001